THE WAVES BEHIND US

BENEDICT KIELY

The Waves
Behind Us

A Memoir

Methuen

Published by Methuen 1999

1 3 5 7 9 10 8 6 4 2

First published in the United Kingdom in 1999 by
Methuen Publishing Ltd,
215 Vauxhall Bridge Road, London SW1V 1EJ

Peribo Pty Ltd, 58 Beaumont Road, Mount Kuring-Gai
NSW 2080, Australia, ACN 002 273 761
(for Australia and New Zealand)

Methuen Publishing Limited Reg. No. 3543167

A CIP catalogue record for this book
is available from the British Library

ISBN 0-413-70160-3

Typeset by Deltatype Ltd, Birkenhead, Merseyside

Printed and bound in Great Britain by
Creative Print and Design (Wales), Ebbw Vale

For Frances

CONTENTS

The light which experience gives is a lantern on the stern which shines only on the waves behind us.

Samuel Taylor Coleridge

The Palace and the Pearl

Do I overpopulate my text and/or my Ireland with poets, playwrights and the like? Well, it may have been my fortune, good or ill, over the years to encounter a fair share of them. Or it may simply be that, as Patrick Kavanagh said, there is in Dublin, at any given moment, a standing army of one thousand young poets.

Mr W. B. Yeats, who was a poet, saw, in 1919, the year in which I was born, he saw, did Mr Yeats, the swan, the image of the soul, leaping into the desolate heaven, and knew that that image could bring wildness, bring a rage to end all things.

Not even every age or epoch, but every generation, every decade in these Gadarene times, has its own image.

When I first settled in Dublin City in 1940, and began to try to write, the echoes of the wings of the departed swan could still be heard in the air above us. Yeats had died, as we all know, in 1939, and I, on the flat of my back in an orthopaedic hospital in North County Dublin, had written a poem, God help us, and happily never published nor ever even offered to anybody for publication, about his passing. So did a lot of other people, including an Englishman, by the name of Auden, write poems on that occasion.

Mobile again, and moving around the streets of Dublin, and in first year in college, I, because I was lucky enough to fall over, you might say, a part-time job on a weekly newspaper, was suddenly catapulted into the most distinguished company: into a group of men all, by the nature of time and the case, older than myself. All that, in the Palace Bar and later in the Pearl Bar, both in Fleet Street and quite close to Anna Livia Plurabelle, was the Dublin literary and artistic scene fifty-eight years ago. The shadow of the Great Swan Himself was still up there, the echo of the beat of the wings re-echoed in the conversation.

The great R. M. Smyllie, then editor of the *Irish Times*, and great intellectually and physically, had called Mr Yeats (on the telephone), to inform him that the Nobel Prize was on the way and Mr Yeats had said: 'Bertie, how much?'

As from one Sligoman to another.

Around Smyllie, and in the Palace Bar, an impressive group had gathered. M. J. MacManus, bibliophile and journalist (as boys, Smyllie and himself had competed on the fiddle at the Sligo Feis Cheoil). Francis MacManus, novelist. The poets Seumas O'Sullivan, Austin Clarke, Pádraic Fallon, Robert Farren, Patrick MacDonogh, Donagh MacDonagh, son of that Thomas MacDonagh, also a poet, executed by the order of General Maxwell in 1916. There was Patrick Kavanagh who had once wished fervently to me that his father had only fought for Ireland for five minutes instead of working for her, and to survive, for fifty years. Brinsley MacNamara, novelist and playwright, quarrelled with Smyllie and withdrew to the Scotch House, then but now no longer on the Liffeyside.

The names of that amazing group then in the Palace, which still survives, are too many to mention. There were painters too – Seán O'Sullivan, Willy Connor, Harry Kernoff and a dozen others – and the faces of most of the gathering were commemorated by the New Zealand caricaturist, Alan Reeve, in a drawing still to be seen and wonderingly inspected: Flann O'Brien or Myles na gCopaleen or Brian O'Nolan (three men, or more, in one), in the middle of it all and casting a cold eye, or six or more eyes.

William Saroyan had visited the Palace and written about it. Then Smyllie quarrelled with a new proprietor and, refreshment in hand, led the entire contingent back along the street to Gus Weldon's Pearl Bar. Cyril Connolly had come calling to lay the ground for a special Irish edition of *Horizon*. Denis Ireland, Joseph Tomelty, John Hewitt and John Boyd and Sam Hanna Bell from Belfast, reported for duty when visiting the other city. Sean O'Faolain looked in very occasionally: and Frank O'Connor, Kate O'Brien, Walter Starkie, Enid Starkie, W. R. Rogers, Louis MacNeice when they were in town, and once, on a wild and most memorable evening, Dylan Thomas. For all I know or remember even Samuel Beckett may have been glimpsed there, towed along, perhaps, by Con Leventhal of Trinity College.

Patrick Kavanagh, after an unfortunate to-do with Brendan Behan, withdrew up the slope to the South (as did the Jacobites on the fatal field of Aughrim), to McDaid's pub, where he held his own court, surrounded, as I've said he splendidly described it, by that standing army of a thousand young poets: and where John Ryan founded and edited the magazine, *Envoy*. Well, not exactly in the pub but in an office in the neighbourhood. *Envoy* joined, if but briefly and for two years, an illustrious company of Irish literary periodicals. There had been *The Bell*, edited by Sean O'Faolain and, later, by that notable warhorse, Peadar O'Donnell. There was *Irish Writing*, edited by David Marcus and afterwards by Sean J. White. There was *The Dublin Magazine*, edited for a long time by the poet, Seumas O'Sullivan, and in its final years, and until costings made life impossible, by John Ryan.

Ryan has well recalled the period in his book, *Remembering How We Stood*, as did also Anthony Cronin, poet, novelist, critic, and tireless worker on behalf of other writers and artists, in his melancholy, humorous, and always brilliant, book, *Dead as Doornails*. And see, also, *The Ginger Man*, by J. P. Donleavy.

It was a vivid, living society, nor do I think that in saying so I am being merely the aged man, a paltry thing, a tattered coat upon a stick, and mournfully praising times past.

Some time in the late 1950s I seemed to sense around me an awesome silence. The Sages standing in God's holy fire as in the cold mosaic of a wall, seemed, genuinely, to have entered into a petrifaction that was more granite than golden. The young sprouts were not surfacing and, as Patrick Kavanagh, recalling his days as a ploughman, thought, the dust of the past had smothered them, 'cursed for being in the way'. As for my bewildered self, I seemed at that time to belong to no particular age group. Three times the then Censorship of Publications had, for three novels, laurelled me for being 'in general tendency indecent or obscene'. Which made me feel more or less respectable. For the dear censors of the time scattered their awards with such a lavish hand on everybody from M. Sartre in Paris to Ernest in Havana, and with special generosity to Irish writers who were *ipso facto* assumed to be blackguards – that a writer here felt rather out of it if he were not banned. The sad institution as good as perished before ridicule and the arrival of television (although there had once been a quite laughable attempt to reactivate it). The last Irish writers to be victimised by it were, probably, John Broderick, Edna O'Brien, Brendan Behan and John McGahern.

But, as I was saying, those decent people had scarcely yet surfaced when I noticed the silence. And round about that time I was asked to write for the London *Spectator*, an article on the state of literature in Ireland among the up-and-coming, and found myself talking something like this: that Brendan Behan might finish that autobiographical book, that Edna O'Brien might write that novel, and so on. As it happened they both did, and more besides, and many other things happened, and the skies brightened and the voice of the turtle was heard in the land.

Among my happy memories of those days is one of walking with Brendan and Edna on the sea front at Clontarf and hearing Brendan enthusing about the lady's literary talent and lovely nature.

Round about the same time Terence de Vere White resigned from a legal career to devote himself to literary journalism and criticism, to the writing of biographies of Isaac Butt and Kevin O'Higgins and the Wildes of Merrion Square, and of Thomas Moore, and to the writing of polished novels and short stories: to become, in fact, one of the last of that race of men of letters of whom John Gross has written so well.

Brian Friel, I knew well, and his father before him, and I may well have been among the first of the general public to know that he had given up a teaching career to devote himself to writing for the stage, with notable results in Dublin, London and New York. The future was also to give to the Irish stage the works of Thomas Murphy, Thomas Kilroy, also a novelist, Brendan Behan himself, J. B. Keane, Bryan MacMahon, Tom MacIntyre, Frank McGuinness and others; and to Dublin, London and New York the work of Hugh Leonard.

Back in those days of my *Spectator* article, Sean J. White had introduced me to his friend, Thomas Kinsella, then working in the Department of Finance, and living in an eyrie of an apartment high above Baggot Street, and beginning to shape perfect poems that one might then have called metaphysical; yet not above relaxing, anonymously, as tradition had it that Goldsmith had done, into a ballad for and about the Dublin streets. White had also brought to my house, then in Clontarf, that half-American young man who came from my own corner of Tyrone and who pleasantly informed me that he would be the writer, and the poet, of the Montagues. His reference was to the fact that in 1936 I had, when the family came back from the States, encountered his elder brother and thought, and said, that that elder brother would be a writer. Instead, he chose to walk in the higher way of medicine. The younger brother, John, one of a set of three brothers, was not talking idly.

Then from nieces and nephews of mine, who were at Queen's University in Belfast, I began to hear much talk of, and had already begun to read, Seamus Heaney. And thus became aware of three strong pillars of the pavilion that now shelters the standing army. The assembly is quite impressive. Perhaps not as numerous as Kavanagh's army. But on a recent count I reckoned fifty-three not unworthy names, men and women of the North and South writing in English and in Irish, some in both. Merely to list the names would be lengthy, and dull for the reader and, on a small island, dangerous for the writer.

One day in the newsagent's here in Donnybrook the lady behind the counter asked me wasn't I supposed to be a writer. I confessed to the supposed to be.

A gracious lady of my acquaintance says that everybody in Ireland is supposed to be doing something or other, so that it well may be that all Ireland is merely a supposition.

But the other lady behind the newsagent's counter went on: 'There are a lot of writers today. There used not to be so many writers.'

What she meant was, I feel, the current exposure of some writers on television chat shows and the much more frequent exposure of other energetic people who write books about moving statues or English spies or professional boxers, or racing cyclists who never see anything except the road below them and the back wheel in front of them: and on other matters of wide public interest.

Yet, looking back from where I now stand and looking also around me, Ireland does seem to me to have been, and to be, blessed, or afflicted, with a large number of people who have persisted, and who persist, in writing it down.

ONE

A Bomb to Begin With

That night, away back in 1941, when the German war-plane dropped the bombs on the North Strand Road and on Summerhill Parade, in north Dublin City, I was living round the corner in my sister Rita's house. I am trying to place myself. If it is of any interest to anyone I was then twenty-two years of age.

But about bombs. From what I heard, and read afterwards, it would seem that the blockbuster that wrecked the North Strand Road, and killed a lot of decent people, passed right over our heads in that part of the city. It certainly seemed so at the time. My own head was out of my bedroom window and never in my life have I heard such an awesome whistling sound in the sky above. Not, at any rate, until I heard my first jet-planes. These were RAF fighters exercising for the fun of it, many years later, over the Wirral in Cheshire. The special whistle, or scream or shriek, of the Angel of Death. It is amazing, and in a way, terrifying to consider how easily we grow accustomed to the weird sounds of our times. And such sounds, and the non-stop noise in which so many of us live, cannot be good for us. Even when it ends up in nothing worse than noise. . . .

That was a warm night in June in 1941, and my bedroom window was wide open. When the German war-plane came over, and the anti-aircraft guns began, my two nephews and myself had our heads out another window so as to watch the fireworks of the bursting shrapnel: as marvellous as anything in China. Needless to say we had not the faintest idea that anybody was going to drop a bomb or we would not have had our heads out the window. Then the earth shuddered as if it had been stopped abruptly in its stride. And a great column of smoke and flame rose up over there in what I would have said, at that startled moment, was the direction of Ringsend and the South Wall. Which seemed logical at that moment in history: the academic theory being that aerial bombers would go for dockside installations.

Bernard Shaw, long ago, knew better than that and said it, when he wrote in *Heartbreak House* that the 'ultimate hellishness of modern warfare would be aimed at the civilian population'. But not even Shaw could foresee the proliferation in our day of the creeping terrorist, the viper and the mad dog in broad daylight and on the crowded street. Perhaps I am being unfair to mad dogs and even to vipers who can kill only one at a time and who, themselves, take a high risk. Long ago when mad dogs ran around the streets slavering with rabies, people could see them and know them for what they were. Oliver Goldsmith, who is two hundred and seventy-one years alive this year, would surely agree.

But, at any rate: Tom Stanley, my brother-in-law, and myself headed off running towards the pillar of fire or cloud or whatever it was. Beyond the canal bridge at the end of Summerhill Parade we were ankle deep in broken glass. Even the basement windows in the orphanage in North William Street had been sucked out by the blast and down there, in the shadows and candlelight, the nuns were calming a crowd of little girls, all chattering like sparrows.

A young journalist, who was later to become a close friend of mine, was to tell me that, on that night, when he pressed button B in a nearby telephone booth to get his money back, he got not his own thruppence (the price at the time for a call) but a shower of broken glass.

Then a man in the uniform of the LDF (Local Defence Force) of the time stopped Tom Stanley and myself at the corner of North William Street and the North Strand. He said that his mother was in there in a half-wrecked house and would we go in with him. But at that moment somebody called to him to say that his mother was safe. Then in the hallway of that shattered house we found another old lady. She was in her nightdress and there was blood on her face. All her worldly belongings, she said, were in there in that room, including three shillings and eightpence in a purse. That was the exact sum she mentioned: three shillings and eightpence.

We went into the room. The dear lady must have left the single bed in the corner of the room when the first bomb, a comparatively small one, fell on Summerhill Parade. Within a few paces of the spot where James Joyce's story 'Araby' begins. And John Ryan, a great Joycean scholar, once pointed out to me that that German bomb on the North Strand Road, in Dublin City, demolished the undertaker's premises that had, in *Ulysses*, dealt with the funeral rites of poor Paddy Dignam. It was difficult, John said, to drop a bomb at all on that part of Ireland and not hit some portion of the Dublin of James Joyce.

And it was a lucky thing for that dear lady that the first and smaller bomb had awakened her. For the blast from the later and bigger bomb had piled everything in the room, and a portion of the ceiling, on the top of her bed. The three-and-eightpence, and the purse that held all that wealth, were gone for ever. Tom Stanley gave her what money he had on him. I had nothing. The LDF man found her a coat and shoes. Then the cordons of army, LDF and fire brigade were all around us and since we wore no uniforms, of any variety, we had to leave the area. And we went: meditating on the Captains and the Kings and on how great German armies marched singing against mighty England, as then was, and how the whole bloody lot of them, English and French and Germans, could leave a frightened, wounded, old lady rooting for a purse and three-and-eightpence in the rubble of a room in North William Street, Dublin City. And more besides. And in many other places.

As Tom and I walked away in a little lane of low houses that led out to Portland Row we saw a young girl in her nightdress helping her grandfather to put the sash back in the window. So I joined in the struggle and, when we had the job done, we noticed that, anyway, there wasn't a fragment of glass left in the damned thing. So we laughed. And the young girl made tea. Such camaraderie was possible, as Londoners well knew at that time, and as the people of many cities were to discover, even though the skies pissed fire.

The deepest evil of the secret bomber may be that he casts a blight on humanity on the very ground he crawls on. A Belfast friend of mine who had lived through the London Blitz once told me that London was then a happy city compared with the sufferings and horror and distrust that marked Belfast over a quarter of a century. But Belfast, which is my second favourite city, had in it for a long time the elements of great unhappiness, hatred and fear. It is a strange and perverse thing that we, the Irish, who were spared some of the worst horrors of our time during the Second World War, should have reared amongst us men who insisted on bringing the horrors home and in an even more dreadful and evil form, because sinister and secretive.

But to alter the mood. That night long ago in 1941 two men stopped me at the corner of Charles Street and told me the almost inevitable story about a third man, their pal, who had slept through it all and never heard a sound.

By a roundabout route we walked home. Groups of people talked nervously at doorways. In Drumcondra Road a man, leaning on his garden gate, told us the story of a chair in his house, in a room with an open window, and the chair, affected by the blast, leaped up and smashed itself against the wall. The Devil himself, he said, could have done no better.

Tom Barry of Cork, a notable guerrilla leader in the 1920s, the happy times of the Black and Tans, lamented in a book he wrote that, in his warrior days, he and his amiable associates knew so little about explosives and the incalculable effect of blast. We all know now. But it took a very big war and then the last thirty years, here, there and everywhere, to teach us. And we are not much the better off for the knowledge.

And anyway: Tom Barry meant to use explosives only against fortifications with armed men behind them, not against the homes and lives of his own people.

But in that part of Dublin City things were happening long before I got there and before the German fellow, whom I never had the pleasure of meeting, dropped the bomb.

For instance: 'North Richmond Street, being blind, was a quiet street except at the hour when the Christian Brothers' School set the boys free. An uninhabited house of two storeys stood at the blind end, detached from its neighbours in a square ground. The other houses of the street, conscious of decent lives within them, gazed at one another with brown imperturbable faces.'

Thank you, Mr Joyce.

That street, I learnedly considered, as in 1940 I walked by the corner, was also the street along which a refined Quaker lady had walked to pay a visit to Gerald Griffin, a Christian Brother who had once been a novelist, a poet and a playwright, and who had had what seems to have been a gentle platonic fluttering with the Quaker lady. And then, in a holy fit of flight from the World, he destroyed what remained of his manuscripts and took off for unalloyed religion. When he was told that the Quaker lady, who was also blamelessly wedded, was in the parlour to pay him a call he gave the matter prayerful thought, sent her a message that he could not see her, and went on being unalloyed.

That crisis of conscience found no place in James Joyce's *Dubliners*. Although Joyce was well aware of it, as he was of almost everything. Perhaps it was that Griffin was not a Dubliner, nor ever could have been. He was a runner-in from Limerick and had left it too late to change into anything else except an Irish Christian Brother. A runner-in may, by endurance and the passage of time, become a Dubliner. So have I found it. But never a Dublinman. There is a subtle difference.

Yet it always did seem to me that it was at least interesting that that moment in the life of Gerald Griffin should have taken place in the same street in which the quest for love and Araby in Joyce's story began, and ended in a boy's disillusion. Those brown, imperturbable faces, and behind them the consciousness of decent lives, looked out on that darkness of agony in which man knows himself 'as a creature driven and derided by vanity'. Brown but perturbed, even outraged, faces, here and elsewhere, looked out on the man who had written 'Araby', and more besides.

Those were odd ghosts to encounter when I was settling, more or less, into Dublin in 1940. North Richmond Street, that sawed-off street, going nowhere and leading nowhere, seemed, because of those ghosts, a natural place of pilgrimage: and the easier to get to because my first tent in the city was pegged down a few minutes' walk away, and across the banks of the Royal Canal, in Ballybough.

Curiously enough, too, the first person I had heard up to that moment, making a favourable, an impassioned, statement on James Joyce, had been an Irish Christian Brother. That had happened during a class in trigonometry in a secondary school in Ulster some time during the 1930s. And the good Brother was given to digression into matters closer to his heart than sines and cosines. Although, long afterwards, that particular digression did not seem as far or as fanciful as it then did. Lots of trig. at Finnegans Wake: as the old Dublin ballad almost said.

That dear Brother was a cultured man with literary tastes, and he defended Joyce to a class of half-comprehending young fellows, not just because Joyce was a great writer but because he was a great Irish writer, a national possession, something to be proud of. And because it was evident from the attitude of certain parties in Britain and the USA towards the great novel, *Ulysses*, that yet another attempt was being made to do the Irish down. That the book had been published and praised in France simply went to show that the most civilised people in Europe were with us as they had been with us in the past: sails cracking in Bantry Bay, if only the luck and the weather had been with us. He could not approve, he told us, of literary criticism by Customs and Excise. The reading of *Dubliners* was, he held, a preparation for walking the streets of the golden city where so many of the great and memorable had been.

For an Irish Christian Brother that was an unusual approach to James Joyce. But then that teacher, whose name was Rice, was a most unusual man and we were lucky to have him. He made us realise that there was a world where books mattered and, also, that all writers were not, as the curriculum assumed, dead. The curriculum, needless to say, made no mention of James Joyce and found room only for a few early poems of William Yeats, who might have been embalmed for centuries for anything the notes to our texts had to say. Albert's *History of English Literature*, then prescribed for secondary schools in the Six Counties of North-east Ireland, told us that Irishmen had often made a fresh and lively contribution but that, as a rule, they were uneducated, uncultured men. The Irishmen whom the historian, Mr or Dr Albert, an English schoolteacher, was then mentioning, in that comment, were Burke, Goldsmith and Berkeley, who clearly might have achieved something if they had only had the benefit of an education.

For our benefit, too, and to relieve his own soul of an indignation, our teacher of trigonometry came down like thunder on a hostile review that a learned, versatile and turbulent professor had written of a book of poetry by F. R. Higgins. And we came to know that learned professors could also be obtuse. And we were treated to a colourful making of comparisons between the poems of Higgins and 'The Love Songs of Connacht'. So that those of his pupils who cared about such things, and who went that way, got to Dublin with their eyes wide open.

Joyce was, then, the writer who proved to whatever was chauvinistic in one that an Irish writer could shake the world. It was also pretty obvious that he was neither uneducated nor uncultured, although Virginia Woolf, God bless the girl, had her own ideas about that. Then he was, in the style of 'scrupulous meanness' of *Dubliners*, the guide to the city. The famous declaratory passage was an interesting parallel to the passage in which William Carleton, an Ulsterman like myself, had taken it upon himself to write the *Traits and Stories of the Irish Peasantry*. William Carleton, coming down to Dublin from my own part of the North, making the journey on foot as Patrick Kavanagh, the poet, was later to do, explained his reasons for writing about his own people:

> I found them a class unknown in literature, unknown by their own landlords, and unknown by those in whose hands much of their destiny was placed. If I became the historian of their habits and manners, their feelings, their prejudices, their superstitions and their crimes; if I have attempted to delineate their moral, religious and physical state, it was because I saw no person willing to undertake a task which surely must be looked upon as a most important one. . . .
> I was anxious that those who ought, but did not, understand their character, should know them, not merely for selfish purposes, but that they should teach them to know themselves and appreciate their rights, both moral and civil, as rational men, who owe obedience to law without the necessity of being slave either to priest or landlord. . . .

So it was that James Joyce, Gerald Griffin, William Carleton, and a learned Christian Brother introduced me to Dublin City. Spread the carpet for the boy littérateur they did, and the best of good luck to them. . . .

Well, not entirely. I fear the introduction was simpler and not quite as splendid as all that. Yet it had its own memorable moments.

Ten years of age I was when I first made the journey. By excursion train and under the care of my father. He was making the trip to visit sisters Rita and Eileen who were already working in the big city and not yet married. My literary mind at the time was more at home with Buffalo Bill than with Stephen Dedalus. There were, also, Deadwood Dick and two fellows called Hashknife and Sleepy. And eminent authors by the names of Zane Gray and W. C. Tuttle. And Ridgewell Cullum. And Edgar Wallace.

The train journey was splendid. A distant glimpse of the Sperrin Mountains, and then the Mountains of Pomeroy, and there was a song about the latter even though they weren't mountains, just smooth green hills. There was Dungannon and the ghost of the great O'Neill who shook his sword at Queen Elizabeth I. There was Portadown and all the Orangemen. Then, far to the left, a hint of the Mountains of Mourne sweeping down to the sea, as they obligingly did to give truth to the words of yet another song.

Seated in the carriage with us was a small man with a big white moustache and a pointy sort of a grey felt hat: Jamie Kyle, the last-but-one town crier from Omagh, my native town. His duties consisted of walking the town and ringing a handbell and crying out the forthcoming of some event considered of importance by the town council. Jamie's knowledge of geography extended little beyond the town and he was certain that the Mountains of Mourne were the Hills of Donegal. My father, who was born in Donegal and who had been to Africa and the Barbadoes and back, was doing his best to enlighten him. With, I felt, little success. We had no map.

Then we came to the great high viaduct over the Boyne at Drogheda. Three men in the coach stood up, hatless, and saluted. They were good Orangemen who, in honour of William of Orange, always acted like that when they crossed the Boyne as he had done, on horseback, in 1690.

And the next thing was we were in Dublin.

How now did I know I was in Dublin?

My father may simply have said: 'This is it. Here we are in Dublin. Even if Jamie there thinks he's in Paris or Cork or Capetown.' But a little later Moran's Hotel told me. This was how. Moran's Hotel in Talbot Street, and the Hellfire Club away up the mountains, were around the first things I ever knew about Dublin. They were a part of my consciousness long before the Post Office and Patrick Pearse and the Rising of 1916 ever were; or the Phoenix Park, or the roofless tram to the summit of the Hill of Howth, or Dalkey or Killiney or . . . even Dolly Fausett's. The hotel, Moran's Hotel, I knew about because a picture-advertisement of it was a permanent vision on the bill-hoardings of the David Allen advertising company of the time: a very large coloured picture with the red-brick portion of the building shining like a splendid sunset. So that when I first came down the long steps from Amiens Street Station, now James Connolly Station, and walked up Talbot Street, still mostly called Talbot Street, and saw all those red bricks, I knew, beyond all shadow of doubt, that I was really and truly in Dublin.

It occurs to me, in passing, that the only advertisements that ever made any impression on me were those great pictures long ago on the hoardings. Of course I was looking at them with young, fresh eyes and believing in all the wonders they promised. And there wasn't that much advertising lying around then. While nowadays our eyes and ears and what brains we have left all suffer from overexposure to the hucksters and pedlars shouting and singing their wares on the fair green on a fair day that never lets up. But who that had any wit ever wanted the fair day to last for ever?

For a ten-pound note now (that is, if that's worth anything nowadays) I couldn't tell you what advertisements were forced on us by the telly last night. But as clear as the light on a good bright morning I can see the stormy ocean, coloured blues and whites that seemed impossible for the ocean even then, and the fat, laughing man in his pyjamas sitting with his legs around the neck of a huge bottle, a big-bellied bottle that always made me think of Robert Louis Stevenson's story, 'The Bottle Imp'. . . . And the lettering on the hoarding told the world that Bovril prevented that sinking feeling.

Or that long-faced, long-legged English gentleman, dressed in tight breeches and a green coat who advertised a splendid brand of marmalade. Because of his pointy chin I always, at an early age, thought he was the Devil: a nice sort of devil but still the Devil, the boss guy, Lucifer, the bearer of light who took the awful nosedive and provided one of the few passages of entertainment in a long poem by John Milton: Lucifer or Thou, whatever title suit Thee, Auld Hornie, Satan, Nick or Clootie.

And as far as poetry is concerned I may, in my declining years, forget a lot of Burns and a lot of Shakespeare and Yeats and Eliot and Auden and others. But never will I forget the advertisement for a soap that I first read on a hoarding on the station-brae in the town I was reared in. The poet said:

> Be you fat or be you lean
> There is no soap like Preservene.

A noble cleansing couplet.

That passing reference to the Devil, God bless him, brings me back, not illogically, to the Hellfire Club. I was interested in it at an early age because of the story that the Devil had appeared there the night the house burned down. Since the eye of childhood does not fear, but delights in a painted Devil, it was the sort of story that stayed in the memory. There was, also, the delightful tale of the group of eighteenth-century Bucks (i.e. sportive and sporting gentlemen) who were driven up there by a Dublin jarvey and who filled him or helped him to fill himself with whiskey until he flowed over, and then set a match to him. Any day nowadays you read worse in the papers of happy events anywhere, in Belfast or Bayreuth or Bosnia or the Bowery, or . . . .

And it may occur to you that, in the old days, only sporting gentlemen behaved like that.

But the Hellfire Club itself I did not see until three years after that first day in Dublin.

So it was that I came to be introduced to Dublin City. And portions of Dublin could not have been unaware of the great event. For this reason. On that day I did a woeful lot of walking. My father was a great man to walk. And proud of it. He had in his time been proud to smoke, drink and chaw tobacco, and tell stories. Under, I suspect, an angelic influence, he gave up the drinking and smoking. He chawed a little for the fun of it, and to display his artistry and good aim. Once he offered me a bite on the twist and the taste of it, I feel, turned me off tobacco for life.

But he never stopped telling stories. He would say: 'I was in South

Africa. Beyond a shadow of a doubt. The Boer War. Never fired a shot. Except one. At a black snake. Never found out whether I hit or missed. But I'll tell you what I did do. For a shilling a day or whatever they paid us. I walked six times round South Africa.'

So he could walk like a well-oiled machine and what could his son do but try to keep up with him. And I did. I was, also, good at walking. But, on that day, I had another problem. So that I should show myself in the Big City in proper style my mother had, two days previously, sent me to the barber. Fair enough. But the barber, a decent man and very polite, had been drinking. And in spite of all my wriggling and protesting, he balded me. In those days little boys in towns held, with some reason, that only country boys were baldy. Their fathers did the dirty trick. Barbers were hard to come by in rural places. So off to Dublin went the baldy boy, clutching his school cap which, as hell would have it, he then lost in the train. And when he stepped off that train, another fearful discovery.

The iron tip on the heel of his left shoe was loose and clinking. Tough enough it was to be a leper but to have to ring a bell about it. Every person in Dublin was looking at and laughing at the bell-ringing, baldy boy from the country. And years later I told the story of my agony to Brendan Behan. Who said: 'You're right. They were. I was there myself. Looking at you. Listening to the bells, bells, bells. And laughing.'

To this day Brendan's fantasy of those two wee boys can move me and I see and hear Brendan alive and laughing.

In the years to come, Moran's Hotel was to be a most pleasant meeting place, at all hours, for hard-working journalists (relaxing behind the red bricks), for members of the Garda Síochána from nearby Store Street Station, and for many normal human beings: all relaxing. It was a placc to meet and make good and useful friends.

And the baldy clinking boy was doomed to be a journalist.

TWO

Staring Yourself in the Face

One of the laws of life is that if you're looking urgently for a book on your shelves then that book, very frequently, is the one book you will not find. You may come across it a week later when you have forgotten why you were looking for it in the first place. And a sub-clause of that law is that if you are searching for a verse in a long poem the one verse you will not find is the verse you are searching for.

So! I have just been through Tennyson's 'In Memoriam', running my forefinger over the first word of each quatrain, searching for a quotation, failing to find it. I refuse to gratify the malicious god, or demon or imp, who controls such things, by going through that process all over again. So I'll quote from memory:

> The infant, new to earth and sky,
> What time its tiny hand is pressed
> Against the circle of the breast,
> Has never thought that: 'This is I.'

> But as he grows he gathers much,
> And learns the use of I and Me,
> And finds: 'I am not what I see
> And other than the things I touch'.

If I have got that correctly it was something of an achievement. For I haven't seen it in print since 1938 which shows you how long it is since I last read Alfred Lord Tennyson's 'In Memoriam'. I have the highest respect for Lord Tennyson but you can't go on reading him all the time. As my son, John Kiely, at the age of thirteen, said to me when he had bogged down in Herman Melville's great book (one of the greatest of all books) and was relaxing with Erle Stanley Gardner: 'Da, there are more entertaining books in the world than *Moby Dick*.'

A lot of Tennyson stays easily in the memory and those eight lines stay with me because they keep tantalising with the question: 'When did you first realise you were yourself?' We've all played that game. It can even be an amusing sort of party game. What is the first thing you remember? My answer always was, and I've given the matter deep thought, that my cousin Patrick Gormley, of Claramore, near Drumquin in West Tyrone, had black, curly hair.

That memory would bring me back more than seventy years to the sunny day when great handsome Patrick carried me across the fields on his shoulders. I had a fine view of the crown of his head. That was about ten miles from the town of Omagh. As a friend of mine said to me not so long ago: 'Most of your life as a writer you seem to have been living in Omagh Town, and on the year you spent with the Jesuits in the woodlands of the County Laois, and on the eighteen months you spent, because of a broken back, in an orthopaedic hospital in Finglas, North Dublin.'

Well, that's not quite true. For I have been in a few other places from here to Oregon and California and back, and for middling distances in other directions. And done other things besides growing up which most of us must do somewhere. But those early twenty-two and a half years, out of a total of eighty come next August, were to me tremendously important. Two and a half being, you might say and say again, periods of reading and meditation and retreat from the world: the other twenty being the portion of a man's life that shapes his reactions to what is going to happen to him during the rest of it.

One day a TV cameraman who was a friend of mine told me that he had only passed through Omagh once and hadn't noticed the high spires that dominate the town and can be seen from a radius of eight to ten miles of the surrounding countryside. It would be possible to pass through without seeing them if you were sitting at the wheel of your car as almost everybody is in the weird world we have lived into. You would still have to be somewhat unobservant or, at any rate, inattentive. So I said sadly to my friend, the cameraman: 'The first time I passed through Omagh it took me eighteen years. And I did notice the spires and a few other things besides.'

Just here I'd like to quote a piece I wrote some time ago about the view from those spires. You can climb a fair way up the inside of them. Or up to their tops on the outside, if you happen to be a steeplejack. This description is to be found in a long–short story of mine called 'Down Then by Derry': a story about a middle-aged man who comes back, with his young son and daughter, to revisit his native town. There's some truth in the story, about myself and some other people. In the writing of fiction you can, at times, begin with an idea, a glimpse, something that's true or something that truth has taught you. Then you add to it or, you might say, it adds to itself. V. S. Pritchett said well that a novel should be allowed to accumulate. You alter it, twist it this way and that to express what you feel to be the deeper truth. Henry James said that the art of fiction was not in telling what happened but what should have happened. Sometimes the two can be very close to each other, sometimes indistinguishable. Here is the view of the town and the river valley as seen from the spires of Omagh. In the story the middle-aged man is remembering something that happened when he was a schoolboy:

> The two tall limping Gothic spires rose high above the hilly narrow streets. Those two spires and the simple plain spire of the Protestant church – that would be Church of Ireland, for the Methodists and Presbyterians did not rise to spires – could be seen for a distance of ten miles. They soared, they were prayers of a sort, over the riverine countryside. . . .
>
> The taller spire was all of two hundred and thirty feet high, thirty of that being for the surmounting cross. To climb up the inside of that spire you went first by a winding stone stairway to the organ loft, then by a steep straight wooden stairway to the shaky creaky wooden platform where the sexton stood when he pulled the bell-rope, then up a series of perpendicular ladders to the place where the two bells were hung, sullen and heavy, but ready at the twitch of a rope to do their duty.
>
> From that eminence, one hundred and fifty feet up, you could look down on everything. The town was almost flat, no longer all humps and hills and high ridged roofs and steep narrow streets. Down there was the meeting place of two rivers, the Camowen and

the Drumragh: a sparkling trout-water, a sullen pike-water. Who could comprehend the differences there were between rivers? Not to speak now of the Amazon and the Seine and the Volga and the Whang-Ho and the Ohio. But even between neighbouring rivers destined to marry and to melt into one. United, the waters of Drumragh and Camowen went on under the name of the Strule, sweeping in a great horseshoe around the wide holm below the military barracks, trampling and tossing northwards to meet yet another river, the Fairywater, then to vanish glistening into a green-and-blue infinity.

Except you were the sexton, or some lesser person authorised by him, you were not, by no means, supposed to be up there at all. Dusty boards, with crazy, dizzy gaps between them, swayed and bent under your feet. Vicious jackdaws screeched. The blue-and-green infinity into which the sparkling water vanished was the place where Blessington's Rangers had once walked, speaking Gaelic, great axes on shoulders. They cut down the trees to make timber for war against Bonaparte, and money to keep Lord and Lady Blessington, their daughter and the ineffable Count D'Orsay, gallivanting.

One day coming home from school alone – that was a time of the day when it wasn't easy to be alone but, with cunning, it could be managed – he had found the door to the foot of the stone stairway open and had taken the chance that it was open by accident. It was. He made the climb. He saw the world. He was alone with the jackdaws and the moan of the wind. Then on the way down the perpendicular ladders he had missed a rung, slipped, screamed with the jackdaws, grabbed desperately and held on. Just about where the sexton would stand to pull the bell-rope he had vomited a sort of striped vomit that he had never seen before. Even in boyhood there was the fear of death.

Nobody, thank God, had ever found out who had thus paid tribute, made Offertory in the holy place. For weeks afterwards he had felt dizzy even when climbing the stairs to his bedroom. . . .

The poet, Eavan Boland, wrote of that story, to my great gratification, as being a praiseworthy portrayal of 'growth, self-deception and loss'. And it may be that those three words could be cut on the gravestones of many men. One way of looking at life is to see it as a process of attrition. But it could also be a process of accumulation, money, or just memories. And the reference, in that passage, to Blessington's Rangers brings me to an old ballad and to shadowy figures of men I have never seen but who have yet haunted me all my life.

The famous Lady Blessington, or rather her husband, had estates in the Strule Valley, north of Omagh. And when there was a boom in timber during the Napoleonic wars they naturally did well out of the cutting-down and devastating of the woods on those estates. But after Waterloo the slump came and the forest rangers, with no work to do any longer, emigrated to Quebec.

In my boyhood there were still traditions of how the forest rangers used to walk, huge men in homespun, speaking Irish, axes on shoulders, in the old potato market in Omagh. In the 1950s Captain William Maddin Scott, of the Mills in Omagh, and notable head of a notable family, showed me, in the corner of a field, the remains of the walls of a woodman's hut. That old potato marketplace, now almost gone out of existence, always had for me its share of unseen presences. Some time in the early nineteenth century some poet, now unknown, remembered the woodsmen in a ballad that returns regularly to my mind, bringing with it all the echoes and the sunlit or lamplit pictures of what was a particularly happy boyhood:

> Thrice happy and blessed were the days of my childhood,
> And happy the hours we wandered from school
> By green Mountjoy's forest, our dear native wildwood,
> And the green flowery banks of the serpentine Strule . . .

So it was not surprising that when I first made an effort to write a novel it should also be an effort to celebrate that river valley. In a public park on the Camowen River before it reaches Omagh, a park called the Lovers' Retreat but known to the liberal soldiers in the barracks by a grosser name, I met, one evening in 1936, a young soldier. We became friendly over the next few months. Then he disappeared for a while and I next met him being escorted from the railway station to the police barracks by two members of the Royal Ulster Constabulary. In the relaxed atmosphere of those days it was possible to stop and ask them what it was all about. It appeared that my pal had deserted from the army and, while heading for the Border at Strabane, had made love to some bits of property that did not belong to him. Like a bicycle, a suit of civilian clothes, and so on. He was very cheerful about it all and was on the best of terms with his captors.

I never saw him again. But I didn't forget him and, even if I have forgotten his name, I can still see him laughing on his way to jail. And round about the Christmas of 1939 I started to write a novel about him under the title of *King's Shilling*. I suppose I could say very grandly that my runaway soldier was the symbol of the pilgrim soul and that I was trying to express something deep about the plight of man on earth. But then I wasn't trying to make him seem to be anything of the sort. I was merely trying to write down the joy I felt in the Strule Valley when the grass meadows were going down in late June or July, according to the weather of the year. So I set my soldier running away along that valley.

There naturally had to be people in the story or it wouldn't be a story at all. And I really did like the original of the runaway soldier, and the effort of trying to get him down on paper was well worth while. The other people came to my mind as easily as the grass grew. They also had grown in that valley. It never occurred to me that the people were any different from myself. Why should it have? But grass and the river and Bessy Bell mountain were different. People passed, they remained.

The only publisher's reader I ever showed *King's Shilling* to told me that he thought it wouldn't succeed because I couldn't make a hero out of a man who was really running away from his duty. He was either being very righteous about the story or very polite to me. He was a quiet, polite sort of man. Then I showed it to Francis MacManus, a great novelist who was to become a good friend. He read it, handed it back to me, and said brusquely: 'It's a long–short story. Cut it to eighteen thousand words.'

I swallowed my indignation as well as I could. And the pathetic *King's Shilling* lay gathering rust and dust while I worked on what became my first novel, *Land Without Stars*, and on another book, *Counties of Contention*, about Ulster political problems from say, 1910 to 1930. And about the need for what we now call community relations. A vague feeling I have that I didn't solve the problems.

Then when Seamus Campbell, a Belfast scholar, was editing *The Irish Bookman* he encouraged me to follow up the advice of Francis MacManus and reduce *King's Shilling* to publishable length. And I did so, and it came down almost exactly to eighteen thousand words. MacManus had an accurate eye.

So the poor soldier that I met so long ago by the Camowen River finally had a chance to show his paces in the pages of *The Irish Bookman*. His story I reread the other day and, do you know, it wasn't half bad. Although whatever happened to the other thirty-two thousand words, or what under God they were about, I do not recall.

By this time you are wondering whatever happened to my cousin, Patrick Gormley of Claramore, and his head of black curly hair. And how I do associate him with my earliest memory of being myself. And how I can make a rough guess at how far that memory goes back. At that long-ago time I was sitting, as I said, on, of all places, Patrick's shoulders so that I had a fine view of the hair on his head. He was walking along a completely green boreen and I can still see, quite clearly, the smooth green surface. We were going to the house in which my mother's mother had just died. That fixes the date, 1929.

Patrick died in the States long afterwards and his brother Joe, a favourite cousin, kept the name going in Claramore and became, as we say, a legend in his own time. Claramore was always a great house for music and singing and country dances, and Joe was a powerful man to sing and had, in his wide repertoire, the ballad by Felix Kearney of Clanabogan, an old friend of my mother, about the Hills above Drumquin. The ballad even mentions Claramore where the Gormleys have been for longer than anybody remembers. A few lines:

> God bless the hills of Donegal
> I've heard their praises sung
> In days gone by, beyond recall,
> When I was very young.
> Then I would pray I'd see the day,
> Before Life's course was run,
> When I would sing the praises
> Of the hills above Drumquin.
>
> When the whins above Drumbarley
> Make the hills a yellow blaze,
> When the heather turns to purple
> On my native, Dressogue braes,
> When the whinstone rocks at Claramore
> Are glistening in the sun,
> Then Nature's at her grandest
> On the hills above Drumquin. . . .

And more to follow.

Balzac, who said nearly everything that was wise, said: 'Are not our feelings written, as it were, on the things about us?'

As a boy I used to glare, literally glare, at myself in the mirror. This would be at odd moments in the small hours of the morning when the rest of the household had gone to bed. As the old song says:

> *Tá bunadh a' toighe in a luighe*
> *A's tá mise liom féin. . . .*
>
> The household are lying down
> And I am alone.

Given hopelessly to the books, I would have been left crouching hopelessly, and reading, by the fire. The only night I ever let the fire go out, because I was afraid to go out into the dark to root for more fuel, was the night I finished reading *The Master of Ballantrae*: one of the only two books that ever gave me the creeps. The other, at a slightly later date, was *The Turn of the Screw*. Bram Stoker's *Dracula* had no effect whatsoever on me, although the corpulent Christian Brother who apprehended me reading it during class, assured me that that very night I would have an attack of what he called 'the collywobbles'. R. L. Stevenson and Henry James could find hell, so to speak, at home. Nor did they need to make journeys into the land of vampires.

But back to that business about staring or glaring into the mirror in the small hours. Everybody does it now and again. And in the case of most of us, and certainly in my own case and for obvious reasons, it means no delight (unlike young Narcissus by the pool) in the beauty or comeliness of physical appearance. You simply look in the mirror and say to yourself, not always in tones of accusation: 'So there you are.' That exercise I found, long ago, had some interest but little illumination. Nothing was achieved in the way of self-analysis and it dawned on me slowly that it may be in contemplation of the things around you that you begin to understand yourself.

So the town and the spires and the river valley, and the places where the mother's people had been from time immemorial, were part of myself and in them I seemed to understand what life might be about. Yet it was not only a question of who you were and where you were, but of how you got there.

My father had come into those Tyrone places as a wanderer, an ex-soldier out of the Boer War, working as a chainman for the 1911 Ordnance Survey. And the chainmen were all old army comrades who wandered the country together and lived and drank hard. So, one Holy Thursday morning, when the settled citizens were off at church, he wandered into an hotel bar in the village of Drumquin looking for a cure of brandy mixed with burgundy. Once, in his memory, I tried it on a Holy Thursday and can confidently recommend it.

But along with his brandy and burgundy he had, on that holy day, a lecture from the girl behind the bar who wanted to know was that any way to behave on a holy day of obligation. He married her. Not on the spot but shortly afterwards. The details of that meeting I heard only on the day of his funeral, and I used them as the basis for a story called 'Wild Rover No More'.

But long before I heard about that meeting, and as I grew older, I found myself, as had my father, becoming more and more possessed by places: the wide bend, say, of the River Barrow before it joins the Nore above New Ross; or a Dublin street in amber, hazy, early-morning light before the monsters of motors are out and you are still free to see the beauty of the city; even the stony canyons and white peaks above the fruit-bearing Williamette Valley in the State of Oregon. And, as my father did, I find myself relating or inventing stories about those places. That may be a primitive Celtic thing: the compilers of the *Dinnseanchas* found a legend in every place-name. Something of that man, my father, and his passion for places I tried to get into a story called 'A Journey to the Seven Streams'. Here's the beginning of it:

> My father, the heavens be his bed, was a terrible man for telling you
> about the places he had been and for bringing you there, if he could,
> and displaying them to you with a mild and gentle air of
> proprietorship. He couldn't do the showmanship so well in the case
> of Spion Kop where he, and the fortunate ones who hadn't been
> ordered up the hill in the ignorant night, had spent a sad morning
> crouching on African earth and listening to the deadly Boer guns
> that, high above the plain, slaughtered their hapless comrades. Nor
> yet in the case of Halifax, Nova Scotia, nor Barbadoes, where he said

he had heard words of Gaelic from coloured girls who were, he claimed, descended from the Irish transported into slavery in the days of Oliver Cromwell. The great glen of Aherlow, too, which he had helped to chain for His Majesty's Ordnance Survey, was placed inconveniently far to the south in the mystic land of Tipperary, and Cratloe Wood where the Fourth Earl of Leitrim was assassinated was sixty miles away on the winding Donegal fjord called Mulroy Bay. But townlands like Corraheskin, Drumlish, Cornavara, Dooish, the Minnieburns and Claramore, and small towns like Drumquin and Dromore, were all within a ten-mile radius of our town. And something of moment or something amusing had happened in every one of them.

The reiterated music of their names worked on him like a charm. They would, he said, take faery tunes out of the stone fiddle of Castle Caldwell. And, indeed, it was the night he told us the story of the stone fiddle and the drowned fiddler, and recited for us the inscription carved on the fiddle in memory of the fiddler, that he decided to hire a hackney car, a rare and daring thing to do in those days, and bring us out to see in one round trip those most adjacent places of his memories and dreams.

It was a good introduction to, at least, Ireland to have a father who was born in Donegal, whose father came from the Maigue valley in County Limerick, and whose grandfather came from Aherlow in Tipperary, where Kielys seem to have originated. And to have a mother, a Gormley from West Tyrone, whose mother came from Glangevlin in the County Cavan where the River Shannon and all the McGoverns come from. And also to have relatives in Sligo, Leitrim and in Dublin City and in Belfast itself. And also to go in the summers to talk Irish among the rocks of the Rosses at the foot of Mount Errigal and by the edge of the open Atlantic.

There were a lot of relatives out there beyond that ocean, and they came on frequent visits and had a lot to say about the USA in the days, not so long ago, before you could cross the Atlantic in a few hours and on the instalment system. It was also a lucky thing, I think, to spend more than twenty years as a newspaperman. That got me out and about and around the country, and to meet a lot of people and to hear a lot of odd stories. For there is this to be said about newspapermen: they can talk shop without being bores because their shop is everybody else's business.

All life, as you look at it and become part of it, may be the mirrors in which you see and find yourself. For the novelist, his novels and the people in them are what he has seen in the depth of the mirror.

George Moore had a theory that Life could tell a better story, and put a better ending to it, than Art could ever manage. He gave as examples the ironic endings of the lives of Tolstoy, Napoleon and Beau Brummell. He was, perhaps, justifying himself to himself for his coming to Dublin in the early years of the century and using some of the notable people of the place and the time, W. B. Yeats, Lady Gregory, Æ or George Russell, the mystical poet or painter from Lurgan, even his own cousin Edward Martyn, as material for his masterpiece: the three semi-autobiographical volumes of *Hail and Farewell*. Yet he knew quite clearly that the most complete portrait he had painted in those three volumes was the portrait of himself. For when he heard that the witty, waspish Sligowoman, Susan Mitchell, was to write a book about him, and when he guessed (naturally) that the book would be in the nature of a reprisal for what he done in *Hail and Farewell*, he wrote to her:

> I am a part of life like Yeats and Lady Gregory, and you have as much right to sketch me as I have to sketch them, and if your book has any value its value will depend on how much of yourself you put into it. . . . When writing about me, write about yourself. I am only a pretext.

So that in the writing of novels and short stories, and in introducing myself, and in trying to introduce the reader to a mixum-gatherum of themes and people, I was still only glaring into the mirror. Were all those invented people only pretexts? Even when I wrote a study of the life and times of William Carleton, our great Ulster novelist of the nineteenth century, was my interest in him whetted simply by his being a Tyroneman, which I also was? And by his being a novelist, which I was trying to be? Does the novelist wander about like a blind man feeling faces, among his own people, searching for himself?

He writes what he thinks about people and the mortal predicament. The sublimest poet can do no more. But the mortal predicament begins with and centres in himself.

The process goes on. At the moment I am looking, in dismay, at another collection of short stories, at three novels in what I prefer to call a state of decomposition, and at three other uncompleted, very uncompleted, works of what we all elect to call non-fiction. What is fiction and what is not? A man goes on living in the hope that some day he may find out for certain.

THREE

The Dove-delighting Tree

In my days in Earlsfort Terrace, Dublin City, when, to put it this way, it was known as University College, Dublin, or You See Dee. . . . (Although a number of charming young ladies might have thought tht Earlsfort Terrace meant Alexandra College which was then on the other side of the street. . . .)

At any rate: in my days in Earlsfort Terrace I was involved, along with some other notable men of learning, in the production of what was described as a Poetry Broadsheet. The distinguished editor and publisher, a good friend by the name of Brendan O'Brien, afterwards retired from the world to live, and teach, in the exact centre of Ireland, or so it is said to be, i.e. the town of Athlone. Where, over the years, he had a lot to do with the promotion of amateur theatre.

But many curious things appeared in or on that broadsheet. And there is one that always comes back to my mind in days of late June sunshine that can have such a miraculous effect on anything that blossoms. It was a poem that another friend, Liam Carlin, who became a distinguished architect, produced, after a poem by St John Perse. It opened like this:

> Halting my horse by the dove-delighting tree
> I whistle a song so sweet.
> Strong faith shall these streams keep
> With the banks that contain them?
> Living leaves in the morning mist
> Fashioned in glory's image. . . .

Dove-delighting tree! I think I can honestly say that over more than fifty years that image has been close to my mind, in the presence of splendid trees and even more acutely in their absence. I think of it every morning when I look out my window. For out there, and overhanging a bus-stop, is a tree, or a blossoming bush grown far beyond the stature normally allowed to it in more orderly parts of the world of gardens. It has blossoms as brilliantly white and, alas, as transient as the North American dogwood.

Those blossoms it scatters over the patch of lawn. Some mornings you would think there had been an overnight snowfall. It scatters them as a sort of benediction and a promise of hope over the people waiting patiently at the bus-stop. And since the queues there frequently contain a lot of young people of varying colours, from a nearby Dominican College, those falling blossoms seem to me to be a special sort of welcome.

Waiting people stand back and study the tree, or giant bush. And one morning I saw a young girl snap off a blooming twig, sniff it with evident pleasure, twist it into her hair and walk on in style. For it smells of orange and even on a busy city road it pleasantly scents the air. It is, I am told, known as Mock Orange or Philadelphus or even as Bride's Blossom. And winter or summer, in leaf and blossom or bare as a walking stick or a blind man's staff, it delights the birds. Not doves exactly, for the doves in this neighbourhood are few and as heavy as cargo planes from, I suspect, eating at the back door of that same Dominican College. They all look like Reverend Mothers in good condition and although occasionally I see one of them in the tree they stay low down on the branches that are able to support them.

But all day long, and in spite of the traffic, the smalle fowle maken melodye there, as Mr Chaucer might have said. And once, and I swear to God I'm telling no lie, I saw in the early morning a linnet paying the place a brief visit. Where it came from or where it went to I have no idea.

> A linnet who had lost her way
> Sang on a blackened bough in hell. . . .

No, no, Ralph Hodgson, that was another linnet and another place. . . .

But mostly sparrows, and sparrows in hundreds, cheerful, noisy, active, aggressive, dispensing their own particular magnanimities of sound: as Mr Yeats might well have put it. A blossoming perfumed bush filled with sparrows would put anybody into good humour. And I observe and I know from my own experience, that for some people it seems to make waiting for buses just that little bit less monotonous.

There's a nephew of mine by the name of Brian who, when he was a lot smaller than he is today, never seemed to be able to get to school on the day of the monthly cattle fair in our home town. His way to the school led across the fair green, known to us in the more Scottish fashion common in Ulster as the Cow Commons. And at the end of the day he was liable to be overtaken, five or six miles from home, helping some mountainy farmer to herd home a few thrawn bullocks. As he frequently explained to his mother: 'I could stand all day looking at a cow.' Later in life he became quite well known for other things than cow-watching or herding bullocks. Yet I think of his cowboys days when I look at that tree. Because I can study it from where I sit, going through the motions of working or writing, or whatever you may politely call it. And I find that I can sit for a long time just looking at that tree and doing no work at all.

It reminds me of a lot of things. Of other trees, logically enough. Of the giant pine of my boyhood in the park by the Camowen River upstream from Omagh Town: the best and easiest tree in the world to climb. It was as simple as walking upstairs. And from away up there you could look down on most of the world that was worth looking at. That tree I put into a story called 'Bluebell Meadow'. But one day, many years ago, I passed that way and the tree was down and only a fragment of the trunk remained.

It put me in mind of the great Gaelic lament for the passing of the Butlers of Kilcash and the felling of the woods on the slopes of Slievenamon:

> *Cad a dheanamuidh feasta gan adhmaidh*
> *Tá deire na coillte ar lár. . . .*

> What shall we do without timber,
> The last of the woods are down. . . .

However, it was not the woodman but Time, assisted by Tempest, laid low my splendid pine.

Or it reminds me of the great sycamore on the Dromore Road that was a halting place on a walk out of my home town. I'd be afraid almost to pass that way now: expanding towns can be cruel to trees.

Or of the great chestnut in the water-meadow between the Cravenagh Road and the Drumragh River from which Gerry Cassidy fell when he was demonstrating to a few of his school friends, myself included, his ideas on tightrope dancing: out and out to the quivering tip of the branch. He was two weeks in hospital but resurfaced and, later in life, survived the Battle of Libya. Barely survived: left lying for hours on the desert sand with a shattered leg which, to the best of his ability, he bound up with fragments torn from his own clothing.

There were and are more and more and many other trees bringing me back always to where I sit working or writing or gazing out the window: and back always to the poem that almost sixty years ago my architect friend echoed from St John Perse:

> Not that a man may not be sad,
> But rising before the radiant day
> And holding prudent communion
> With the wise shadows of an old tree,
> Leaning his chin upon the last star,
> He sees, deep down in the fasting sky,
> Great things and pure that change to ecstasy. . . .

So from where I sit and write and think (I hope), Earlsfort Terrace and all its ghosts, myself included, are a mile away to the left hand and the north. And in the blessed neighbourhood of St Stephen's Green. I look to the east and the rising sun like King Cormac MacAirt who wished to lie in a Christian grave at Rosnaree on the banks of the Boyne where he had first encountered an immigrant by the name of Patrick MacCalpurnius. And taken, Cormac had, not the soup but the holy water. And I will try to recall my days and years in college and some of the good people I there encountered.

In my home town there was a good, quiet, thoughtful man who thought that if you went to a university you stayed there for a long time. That was because a famous local boy, footballer, fisherman, gambler, boozer, had gone off to become a medical doctor and took a long time about it. Became a chronic medical student but did in the end become a doctor. So for many years and any time I visited my home town that gentle old man would say to me thoughtfully: 'Still at the university, Benny.'

FOUR

UCD

One day in 1944 or 1945 Peter O'Curry said to me: 'Do you remember that paper on G. K. Chesterton that you read in 1940 to the Literature Society in Earlsfort Terrace?' That society was known for short as the English Lit. and was then, and still may be if it still exists, an abode of pastoral peace when compared and/or contrasted with the scenes of public riot in the Literary and Historical Society: the El and Aitch. Which I once heard referred to by my friend, Denis Meehan, who was given to puns, as the Hell and Itch.

Now for several reasons I remembered that paper on G. K. Chesterton. It represented my first effort ever to deliver a formal public address. It was read out loud to a tolerant audience when, three to four years after I had departed from secondary school I found myself, a bit bewildered, in University College, Dublin. Those three to four years had been spent partly as a clerk in the British Post Office, partly as a Jesuit novice, partly (for eighteen months) in an orthopaedic hospital, where I had any God's amount of time to read. So that you could say that I was an odd class of a First Arts student.

Then, in so far as I know, the delivery of that paper provided the only instance of G. K. Chesterton ever helping a young fellow in Ireland to get a job. Already I had one job, with the great and good Capuchin, Father Senan Moynihan, and a retainer, which was good money at the time, for writing articles for *The Father Mathew Record* about all sorts of interesting people, ranging from Monsignor John

O'Connor, who was the model for Chesterton's Father Brown, to Robert Speaight, the actor, who had played in Eliot's *Murder in the Cathedral* and had just then written a book about Hilaire Belloc.

And about Delia Murphy, great lady and lovely singer and her wonderful husband, the diplomatist, T. J. Kiernan. The world was about that time beginning to describe such articles or essays or whatever as profiles.

For a young fellow in 1940 to have one job was something of an achievement or a stroke of luck. There could be no exact description of what it was like to have two jobs. I was a bloody pluralist and still a mere student. And the number of men, later to be distinguished in Church and State, who borrowed from me and repaid when possible (because nobody else had a job at all) the odd sixpence or shilling or half-crown was amazing and gratifying. Never since have I had such a feeling of largesse. And this was how G. K. Chesterton helped to bring it about. For when I promised or threatened to read this paper, to be called 'Enter Mr Chesterton', the secretary of the society, a lovely English girl called Denys Murphy, went down to the offices of the then weekly *Standard* and asked the editor, Peter O'Curry, to act as chairman: an excellent editor and an excellent chairman who afterwards employed me on his newspaper to the great benefit, needless to say, of scholarship, journalism and Chestertonianism.

What that paper was about I can now, you may be glad to hear, in no ways remember. It was succeeded, in the following year, by a paper called 'American Movement and William Saroyan'.

American Movement! Now there was one to puzzle even the professors. And never having, at that time, been next or near the United States I, of course, knew all about it, whatever it was. It implied, I suspect, some connection between what Saroyan himself called Razzle-Dazzle, that whole joyous fall-in-and-follow-the-band quality which is one aspect of American life, and the opening passage of Stephen Vincent Benét's long poem 'Western Star', the one that begins:

> Americans are always moving on,
> It's an old Spanish custom gone astray,
> A sort of English fever, I believe,
> Or just a mere desire to take French leave,

I couldn't say, I couldn't really say.
But when the whistle blows they go away. . . .

As you may readily work out, I am quoting, and inaccurately, from memory.

The discovery and celebration of Saroyan was then a sort of fever with a few of us, all of us at about the age when you can easily get enthusiastic about any writer. A little later it was to be Graham Greene and a later generation of the English Literature Society was to be treated to a paper by a good man called Andy Flynn, and entitled delightfully 'Three Studies in Greene'. It dealt with Graham Greene, Henry Green of *Loving* and similarly named novels, and F. L. Green who wrote *A Fragment of Glass* and *Odd Man Out* and who now seems to be completely, and quite unfairly, forgotten.

What a pity that no way was ever found of preserving the papers read to that society by a most extraordinary list of enthusiastic young pedants. Flann O'Brien's *At Swim-Two-Birds* was then already providing a sort of *lingua franca* for the intellectuals who held up the wall in Main Hall, in Earlsfort Terrace. After all they were only talking about their predecessors: Brian O'Nolan (Flann O'Brien) himself, and Niall Sheridan and Donagh MacDonagh. Frequent references were heard to Flann O'Brien's character, the Pooka McPhelimey, a member of the demon class, who acquired respect by the treatment meted out to his wife who was one of the Corrigans of Carlow. And to that mythological hero who was physically so large that three fifties of fosterlings could engage at handball against the wideness of his backside which was large enough to halt the advance of an army through a mountain pass.

As for William Saroyan, he had visited Dublin some time around 1939, and been in the Palace Bar where all the gods then gathered under the supervision of Jove himself, the (mentally and physically) great R. M. Smyllie, editor of the *Irish Times*. From the list of the names of the people Saroyan recorded that he met there it might seem that some jokers were not above signing themselves by names that were, fair enough, part of Irish history, but whose real possessors were no longer, in all truth, in the land of the living. But it is of interest that when *At Swim-Two-Birds* first appeared the first two notable men to welcome it outside Ireland were Graham Greene and William Saroyan.

Having disposed of William Saroyan in the English Literature Society I turned, the next year, to the formidable bulk of Thomas Carlyle. Dear God, the enthusiasms of the young and innocent! A friend recently posted to me a copy of the *Irish Ecclesiastical Record* for April 1946, in which my paper on Carlyle was printed as were, in other issues, the papers on Chesterton and Saroyan. That was, once again, thanks to Peter O'Curry who, because of his contacts with the reverend editor of the *Record*, had found a market for such oddities. And I would have all who, in 1999, think that Irish writers are overpaid and privileged, know that in 1946 the *Record* paid five guineas for each of those articles. Guineas, as Terry Ward, a great journalist, in Fleet Street, London, used to say: 'Guineas for Gentlemen.' That was good money then, and it is quite certain that the rates of writers' pay have not, in fifty golden years, risen as has the price of wine. Which was also once supposed to be for gentlemen, rich or poor.

Thomas Carlyle I discussed quite frequently at that time with a decent member of the Dublin Communist Party who used to make speeches at the corner of Cathal Brugha Street. My communist friend somewhat oddly considered Carlyle's *The French Revolution* as an encouragement to revolution anywhere. But he did share Hilaire Belloc's opinion that Carlyle could actually make you see what happened in France at that most momentous time. So I turn now to the printed version of that old paper not to read myself, heaven forbid, but to read some of the Carlyle I quoted, and see if I can revive an old enthusiasm.

Sovereigns die and Sovereignties: how all dies, and is for a Time only; is a 'Time-phantasm, yet reckons itself real!' The Merovingian Kings, slowly wending on their bullock-carts through the streets of Paris, with their long hair flowing, have all wended slowly on, – into Eternity. Charlemagne sleeps at Salzburg, with truncheon grounded; only Fable expecting that he will awaken. Charles the Hammer, Pipin Bow-legged, where now is their eye of menace, their voice of command? Rollo and his shaggy Northmen cover not the Seine with ships; but have sailed off on a longer voyage. The hair of Towhead (*Tête d'étoupes*) now needs no combing; Iron-cutter (*Taillefer*) cannot cut a cobweb; shrill Fredegonda, shrill Brunhilda have had out their hot life-scold, and lie silent, their hot life-frenzy cooled. Neither from

that black Tower de Nesle descends now darkling the doomed
gallant, in his sack, to the Seine waters; plunging into Night: for
Dame de Nesle now cares not for this world's gallantry, heeds not
this world's scandal; Dame de Nesle is herself gone into Night. They
are all gone; sunk, – down, down, with the tumult they made; and
the rolling and the trampling of ever new generations passes over
them; and they hear it not any more forever.

FIVE

Oh, Woman of Three Cows

A lady fair in a garden walking
When a well-dressed gentleman came riding by.
He stepped up to her, all for to view her.
And he said: 'Fair lady, would you fancy I?'

There's another version of that ballad and it begins: 'There was once a maid in a lonely garden.' And in which the gentleman arrives, not riding but walking by, and in which, instead of merely fancying the fair lady or suggesting to her that she might fancy him, he actually suggests matrimony.

For me the two versions of the ballad link up two men: one of them that great scholar and collector of ballads, Colm O'Lochlainn, publisher also and proprietor of the Sign of the Three Candles in Fleet Street, Dublin City. And the other man, my cousin, Joe Gormley of Claramore, a farmer, a man in a million to sing ballads and old lavender-sentimental songs. And a man much in love with the land he walked and worked on. They had, each of them, his own version of the story of the lady fair in a garden walking – or of the maid in a lonely garden – and, for the life of me, I can never make up my mind as to which version I prefer.

Colm I first heard and listened to when I was here in Earlsfort Terrace, University College, Dublin. His lectures in and on the native language were a superb entertainment, the like of which no student could hope for under the name of education. He could be talking about the stories of Tomás Bairéad, and very good stories they were and are, but his digressions were always greater than the ostensible topics, and could range from the intimate scientific details of the distilling of poteen to the ballad about Donnelly and Cooper and their great boxing match on the Curragh of Kildare. And then a pause while he'd raise a hand and rub his forehead and smile with bright eyes and say: 'Jack Butler Yeats told me that he had painted a picture of Donnelly and Cooper. But I looked at it for a long time and could find neither Donnelly nor Cooper.'

Then I came to know Colm very well through a sort of Gaelic club called the *Craobh Rua* which may have been founded by the novelist, Liam O'Flaherty, and which was then being maintained mostly by Roger McHugh, playwright, historian and also on the faculty in UCD. And some of Roger's faithful followers, myself included. The club met by night like Christ and Nicodemus, in the premises of the Country Shop in Stephen's Green, and many interesting things happened there: including, one night, Patrick Kavanagh's public declaration of his intention to abandon Ireland for Spain. He never did do so, but stayed his departure until he left for a happier land than Ireland or Spain. But that, as I remember, was a most dramatic night in the Country Shop and involved much solemn and impassioned discussion on the place of the poet in Irish society. We too had many pretty toys when young, as the other Mr Yeats said.

Later still, I had practically a daily meeting with Colm when the two of us lived on Rathgar Road. And one day I went to see him in his office (he was also a select publisher) at the Sign of the Three Candles in Fleet Street, to ask him if he had the music that should go with James Clarence Mangan's 'Oh, Woman of Three Cows'. Now that, indeed, might seem an odd thing to be looking for. As if I had been going to adopt it as my party piece:

> Think of O'Donnell of the Ships,
> The Chief whom nothing daunted.
> Think how he fell in distant Spain,
> Unchronicled, unchaunted.
> He sleeps the great O'Sullivan
> Where thunder cannot rouse.
> Then ask yourself should you be proud,
> Oh, Woman of Three Cows.

But this was my reason for looking for the music. At that time I was writing the script for a radio programme of *The Songs of Young Ireland* (1848 and thereabouts). The songs were sung by the Radió Éireann Singers, conducted by Hans Rosen, a most amiable and distinguished German. And a very pleasant experience it was to be working with such wonderful people. The previous programme of the sort had been on Moore's *Melodies* and had been scripted by Brinsley MacNamara who was always very joyous about the length of time (more than a year) his programme ran.

'Curious thing, you know,' he used to say with great glee, 'that Moore and MacNamara should run together so long in harness.' To Brinsley all life was a curious thing: and rightly so, as most of us are sadly, or comically, aware.

With *The Songs of Young Ireland*, Thomas Davis and James Clarence Mangan and the poets and patriots of 1848, I followed on, and did my best to last as long as Brinsley had done. But I failed. Even though we all did agree that it was legitimate to regard the tradition of the Songs of Young Ireland as beginning with William Drennan's 'When Erin First Rose from the Dark-Swelling Flood', or 'The Wake of William Orr', and coming right up to Francis A. Fahey and 'Oh, My Boat Can lightly Float', and so on. Mangan, of course, was at the centre of the business, and thus the demand for the music to set singing 'Oh, Woman of Three Cows'.

And Colm and myself are standing in the ante-room, or whatever, of his publishing house, and the door open to the street outside. A poet, a gentle man and a Galway man by the name of Kevin Faller, who was Colm's personal secretary, was also in the room, sitting quietly at his desk in a sheltered corner.

So Colm says: 'Easy to find the tune. Or the melody. Or the movement. Or what-you-will. You hear it every day on the radio. All about Ghost Riders in the Sky. But the original was a tune that went with a dance called "My Love is in America".'

And he began to lilt, speeding up the Ghost Riders until they were really galloping, and then he began to foot it to the music and before I knew what I was at, I was leaping around with him. Until at the height of the movement he clapped his hands loudly, paused in his circling, laughed in great style, and said with resonance: 'That meant he slapped her on the backside as they swung in the dance.'

Then an odd silence descended on the room. At his desk in the sheltered corner the poet, Faller, raised his eyes to heaven. And I wheeled around and saw, standing in the open doorway, and they quiet and prayerful, the two most solemn Reverend Mothers that were ever let out of the convent for the day. They were the genuine old-style article and not in the least like the young ladies you see nowadays trotting through Donnybrook on the way south to Belfield where you may now find University College, Dublin.

What those two great, religious ladies ever thought of the cavortings of Colm O'Lochlainn, professor and publisher, and myself, we never did find out. But the whole episode added up to one of those inconsequential moments that can stay in the memory for ever and set you laughing long after they have ceased to be funny, if they ever were, to you or anybody else.

Colm O'Lochlainn and my cousin, Joe Gormley of Claramore, never encountered. But when it came to song and dance, and the music that goes with them, they had a world in common. And, for me, they are for ever bound together by that song about the maid in a lonely garden, or about the lady fair in the garden walking. And about the high moment when the well-dressed gentleman made his splendid proposal:

> Oh, do you see yon high high building?
> And do you see yon castle fine?
> And do you see yon ship on the ocean?
> They'll all be thine if thou wilt be mine.

SIX

In the Long Whispering Corridor

To get backstage in the Abbey Theatre and, also, behind the scenes in Radió Éireann, and to do all that in one week, was not a bad achievement for a young fellow who had but recently come for his first year to University College, Dublin. This was how I came to be backstage at the Abbey.

Brian O'Higgins, the celebrated actor, I had come to know well. Because I had, as far back as 1937, become friendly with two of his brothers and, through them, was privileged to know the whole family and to call at their house. And to be happy in the presence of his father, Brian, a quiet and pleasant man who had come close to the British firing squad at Easter 1916. And to discuss Chesterton with the daughter, Nuala, who had read any God's amount of the Fat Man, and who, afterwards, became a nun.

And in this house I first met a lovely, old, silver-haired lady, Teresa Brayton, who had written, among other matters, that classical, sentimental song about the Irish exile, 'The Old Bog Road':

> My feet are here on Broadway
> This blessed harvest morn,
> And oh, the ache that's in them
> For the spot where I was born. . . .

And also in that house I heard the fine singing of Jimmy Broe, who died young, and talked with Jimmy's mother, Treasa Ní Chormaic,

who had been a famous harpist and who had broadcast from 2RN
(Radió Éireann) in the days of the renowned Seamus Clandillon who
was prepared to fight, literally, in defence of Irish folk music. There
was a story that on one famous day Clandillon took off his coat and
squared up to Colonel Fritz Brase, who happened to be a German
though he was the conductor and instructor of the Irish Army Band,
because the German had spoken disrespectfully of Irish folk music.

The great Clandillon I never saw but I did hear him. And I knew
his son who told me that when the family lived in a certain sea road
in Clontarf they had a poltergeist or something in the house. That
story I afterwards heard confirmed by Robert Brennan who, as well as
having been a 1916 veteran, and an Irish ambassador to Washington,
and a director of Radió Éireann, was also an authority on haunted
houses. There could be some connection between poltergeists and
pipe music and Ariel, the spirit of broadcasting, who can, according to
Shakespeare, girdle the earth so easily and rapidly and so many times.
But Seamus Clandillon's pipe music had faded into the past, and
what I now associate the first director of 2RN with is his splendid, and
the best, translation of 'Sliabh na mBan':

> The French, they say, are in the bay now,
> The tall mast tapering on each gallant ship.
> They'll make a stay now in our green Erin,
> For that's the tale I hear on every lip. . . .

That, as you may readily see, was a multiple digression. And there
may be many such in casual, haphazard memories of forty or so years
going in and out of RE and RTE. But to come back for the moment
to Brian O'Higgins, the son, and the Abbey Theatre.

One day, Brian, the son, knowing with great professional good
humour that I had once starred with the Omagh Players in Padraic
Gregory's *The Coming of the Magi* as Annas, the High Priest, in Acts
One and Two. And in Acts Three and Four, one of the Magi: the
yellow one. Brian, I say, thought that I would like to see the Abbey
backstage and said: 'Come back some night and see what goes on.'

What was going on, in fact, was a party. A beautiful brunette actress
and, afterwards, a very famous one, was going off next morning to
marry a young actor. Everyone was drinking happiness to them and,
in the way theatre people have, the actress was kissing happiness to

all. So I shared in the drink and stood in line to be kissed with the best of them: standing, as far as I recall, right beside the great actor and most wonderful man: F. J. McCormick. It was a memorable experience.

Backstage in Radió Éireann was a little different. But also memorable. A friend of mine, married to a relation of mine, knew an important official in the radio station who had promised that some night he would show my friend and his wife around. It was located in the most historic General Post Office, from the attic (upper floor) of which all our broadcasting was then done. So I went with them and, for the very first time, stepped in at that side door from Henry Street and, using the stairs – because the elevator was, as it so often was, out of order – ascended to look down and walk along that longest corridor in Ireland. Come to that, I don't recollect having seen a longer corridor anywhere else. But I'm not much of a travelled man and there may well be many longer corridors in Russia or in China Herself.

Perhaps my thoughts as I walked along that corridor were on the shouting and burning and destruction of 1916 and on the possibility that there might still be a few ghosts there. The corridor was very quiet: not at all as I was to see it many times afterwards, busy with people darting like rabbits out of one office and into another, or with cultured groups standing at doorways and talking of everything on the earth, or, as became them and their vocations, on the air. Then up the narrow stairs and into a large room, with a large table and chairs, and a grand piano and idle music stands, and we were left there to sit looking through glass at the poet, Patrick Kavanagh.

He was, although you would never have thought it to look at him, reviewing books: he looked more like Cuchulain warring with the relentless waves. He was, I think, quite unaware that he had spectators. But not an audience, because the sound was not coming through to us. He waved his arms. He shuffled his shoulders. He roared at Ireland. To look at him in that glass cage one would never have thought, as I was afterwards to discover, that he could be gentle, childlike, amiable, understanding, even if few men ever worked harder to disguise their virtues than he did. He was a variable man.

Frequently you'll remember people as you first saw them and, for me, Paddy Kavanagh is still in a glass box. Not as he was when he used to sit punditising serenely in the office of the *Standard* in Peter O'Curry's days at the corner of Pearse Street and Tara Street. He owed a lot to Peter and acknowledged that in a dedication. For Peter had written the first news story ever about Paddy: in the *Irish Press* in late 1936 or early 1937. And I had read it in Omagh post office where I was then a sorting clerk and telegraphist.

Not as he was on the day when, with the expression of a schoolboy timidly presenting an essay to a censoring teacher, he handed me a sheet of paper and said: 'Could we sing that to the air of "The Dawning of the Day".'

And I read, written in pencil:

> On Raglan Road on an autumn day I saw her first and knew
> That her dark hair would weave a snare that I might some day
> rue. . . .

We raised our voices in splendid cacophony. It gives me an odd feeling still to think that, after the poet himself, I may have been the first person ever to see that song written down. At that time I was also in college with the beautiful young woman who had inspired the words. Like the poet, we all worshipped from a distance.

Nor even as he was the night a crowd of us toured a series of pubs boldly trying to sell a pair of sandals the poet had cobbled for himself. But cobbled them too big even for his feet, and he had a fine foot. Tomás Ó Duinn, an eminent Gaelic journalist, was of the party, and Kevin B. Nowlan, small in stature but a gigantic historian, and a soldier called Connolly from Boston, and a man called Canito, from Marseilles. No man did we find with feet to fill the sandals. But as we turned the corner at Vincent's Hospital a man, God rest him, dropped dead and, as we carried him into the hospital, we could not help noticing that he had the biggest feet any of us had ever seen.

No: because of my first visit to Radió Éireann, Patrick Kavanagh, the poet, sits for me for ever in a glass box, a saint in a shrine, waving his arms, roaring at Ireland. And it was because of Peter O'Curry that I made my next visit to Radió Éireann to sit in a glass box and do a bit of roaring on my own account.

Under the name of Manus O'Neill, the novelist, Francis MacManus, who meant so much to Radió Éireann and to a lot of people there and elsewhere, was in the early forties writing a weekly column in the *Standard*. Once, since I settled for good or ill in Dublin City, I had seen MacManus. For whom I already had a respect that was to grow over the years and develop into deep friendship. And, as in the case of Kavanagh, I still see him as I first saw him: walking, on one windy day, under Henry Grattan's outstretched arm in College Green. His hands in the pocket of a light raincoat. His head tilted sideways as if he were seeing, somewhere up in the running clouds, one of the old walled gardens of Norman Kilkenny.

He was a Norman man who liked strong, smooth-flowing streams and sunlight on old stone walls. Peter O'Curry introduced us. And one day MacManus said to me: 'Bob Farren would like you to review some books.' Which was how I came to meet Roibeárd Ó Faracháin whose poetry I already knew from the publication of his collection *Thronging Feet*. And I became friendly with two men who for so long were so large a part of Radió Éireann.

Those first reviews were memorable – to me, that is – or perhaps forgettable. What the books were, I most certainly do not remember. This was how it worked.

In those days there weren't many security precautions at the door in Henry Street and, happily, little or no need for such precautions. Although I seem to remember that some foaming patriots did once rush in and, before they could be cut off, shout something or other into a microphone. But the average citizen, or performer, sailed in easily. And not only can I not remember anybody challenging me on that first particular night, but I can't remember anybody directing me to where I was to go. There must, of course, have been somebody, because I found myself in a glass box and breathing into a perforated saucepan. And I knew when to start and I finished when I was finished – if you know what I mean!

Then out I walked and saw no sign of life, no mortal being between the saucepan and the door. Down O'Connell Street I walked, feeling, I fear, a little pride which, however, after a little while, began to evaporate. Because, since nobody afterwards had told me, how did I know I had been in the right place, how did I know that I hadn't been talking into the wrong perforated saucepan? How did I know that Ireland had even heard what I had to say?

So I went into the Oval Bar, to begin with, and into this bar and that bar, hoping that someone would turn to me and say: 'I heard you on the radio [or wireless] tonight.' The thoughts of youth are long, long thoughts. How, for instance, did I know that I had actually been on the air? Nobody in the station had told me so.

These may now seem, to myself and to anybody else, as unreasonable doubts. But they did not seem so at the time. And I was just about ready to ring up relatives in the country who might have been listening in, when I came to the White Horse on the Quays and a man I'd never seen, before nor since, said to me: 'I was listening to you a while ago. Very good. Very distinct.' It was a mistake, and perhaps uncivil, not to ask him who he was: because his was the first voice ever to tell me that I was a broadcaster. On the other hand, perhaps he was an angelic visitant and might not have wished to reveal his name.

That was a long time ago, and broadcasters, veterans or novices, no longer use that door in Henry Street. Spacious palaces have been built on pastures new and to the south and beyond the River Dodder. And technicians sit before control panels that would make the cabin of an airliner look simple. But one day not so long ago, to see a friend well known in the Department of Posts and Telegraphs, I entered by that revered and ancient doorway, in which, going and coming, I had met so many remarkable people, to be politely but sharply challenged by the man in uniform. For the first time in many long years I was unknown in that place.

The first time, I feel, that I ever became conscious that broadcasting might prove to be an important part of the lives of all of us was when I heard the story about the man in Broughderg, in the Sperrin Mountains, who owned one of the first wireless sets in that part of the world in the early 1930s. He didn't get much use of it himself because all the neighbours kept dropping in, twisting knobs and listening with wonderment to the voices and languages of Europe echoing in remote glens where Hugh O'Neill had, a long time ago, trained his swordsmen. Once the man of that house became especially irritated because, when he was trying to listen to somebody in Dublin playing the fiddle, a neighbour's son twisted the knob, filled the house with a ferocious blast of German, and said complacently: 'That's Berlin.'

'Birl Out!' said the owner. And in a fury cleared the house.

So the young fellow responsible put it about that, anyway, it wasn't much of a wireless because it said that last Tuesday's weather would be fine and it poured bullock-stirks all day long.

Vatic properties, you might say, were attributed to the machine itself. And on the night that Lindbergh reached Orly the whole of the town that I was reared in was vividly aware that the wireless had come to stay. Even if wireless sets were still, at that time, rare enough possessions. But Davy Young, a confectioner and greengrocer who had his premises right in the centre of the town, had, also, a wireless set and a throng of enthusiasts who listened to it. The news that the newspapers could not normally cater for, at inconvenient times of the day in the provinces, was written in bold hand on a sheet of paper by one of those enthusiasts and pasted in the window of the shop. And, as a little fellow indeed, standing before the window and reading that a lone man had flown the Atlantic and passed over Ireland in the process, I was vaguely aware that, as they say, history was being made.

To come to less earth-shaking matters. It was my Aunt Kate Gormley of Claramore in south-west Tyrone – a splendid dowager known to half the countryside as Aunt Kate – who made the first family contact with the radio station in the General Post Office in Dublin. The relevant programme was *Ireland is Singing*, presented by the poet, Donagh MacDonagh. And in any survey of the revival of folk balladry in contemporary Ireland both that programme and the recordings made by Delia Murphy in the 1940s deserve a most important place. People from all over the country sent ballad rarities to MacDonagh, and my Aunt Kate's contribution was a piece of caviare about a man who, some time in the nineteenth century, broke out of Omagh jail. That jail – some fragments of it are still to be seen – stood on a steep bluff above the River Strule, and went out of business a long time ago. It is remembered, when and if, for the hanging there, in the early 1870s, of Montgomery, the police inspector, who murdered his friend, Glass, the banker, in Newtown-stewart. There's another and quite fearful ballad about Montgomery's death-cell repentance. And, as I have written elsewhere, the tradition was that, on the morning of his execution, there was such a dreadful thunderstorm that in Omagh to this day, and to the farthest corners of what I once heard Elizabeth Bowen refer to as Lower Ulster, any unusually heavy thunderstorm may still be called Montgomery's Thunder.

> Dark and dismal is the sky,
> And thunderstorms prevail.
> These lines I write, for my last night
> I lie in Omagh jail.
> Lonely here in silent prayer,
> In my dungeon cell,
> Dear wife, to you I bid adieu
> And all my friends farewell.
>
> I feel the rod to face my God
> As from life to death I pass.
> With grief I own the widow's son
> Murdered William Glass.
> Cursed gold, the root of evil,
> Has proved my destiny.
> This day I die in Omagh jail
> Upon a gallows tree.

That was not the ballad that Kate Gormley sent to Donagh MacDonagh. Nor among my disorderly files can I find a copy of the one she did send. But years later Donagh remembered it and talked about it, and Aunt Kate's contribution did give us all an added interest in Radió Éireann. And, perhaps, it was not a coincidence that my first long haul in the way of a series of programmes some years later, *The Nine Counties of Ulster*, should have been based on Ulster folklore and balladry. But not at all, thanks be to God and His Blessed Mother, on politics. C. E. Kelly and Roibeárd Ó Faracháin and Francis MacManus and Seán Mac Réamoinn were responsible for getting that programme off the ground. And it ran for a long time, indeed almost equalling (for longevity) the record for programmes of that sort which, as I mentioned earlier, was set by Brinsley MacNamara when he went on and on for ever with the Radió Éireann Singers and their German conductor, Hans Waldemar Rosen, with their programme on Moore's *Melodies*.

In fact Philip Rooney, who could adapt a novel for radio while you'd be looking at him and who was very close to Brinsley, suggested genially one day to that great man that the programme had lasted for so long that it was suspected that Brinsley was composing melodies, and writing words to go with them, that Thomas Moore had never heard of. It was an idea that delighted Brinsley who had that sort of sense of humour.

But *The Nine Counties of Ulster* gave me the opportunity to work with and really get to know Seán Mac Réamoinn. We had known each other before that. But this was total co-operation and our range was wide. The famous recording vans in which, it had jokingly been said, that Mac Réamoinn and Seamus Ennis and Ciaran MacMathuna invented Irish folk music, had already proved their worth on the two islands and, if I mistake not, on the mainland of Europe. And the net Seán Mac Réamoinn spread over the Nine Counties of Ulster swept in everything from Paddy the Cope in the rocks of the Rosses to an Orangeman in Coalisland, County Tyrone, singing 'The Sash My Father Wore'. (It was possible then to sing the 'Sash' without offence to anybody.)

And from the original ballad about Rody McCorley, about Toome in Antrim in 1798 (not the well-known song by Ethna Carbery) which we afterwards passed on to that great scholar in balladry, Colm O'Lochlainn. And to a rarity called 'Bonny Wood Green', which Seán picked up from a young fellow in Ballymena, County Antrim. And from the story of the above-mentioned Newtownstewart murder, about which Philip Rooney and Denis Johnston had written radio plays and which, over the years had become encrusted with weird barnacles of folklore, to equally weird tales about Father MacFadden and the Gweedore evictions.

It was a rare experience to explore my home province of Ulster with a man who came to it with a fresh eye and a relentless energy. Like a cunning prospector facing into barren Nevada hills, he divined and found precious metal in the most unlikely places. The story of 'Bonny Wood Green' is a case in point.

In Ballymena Town, a young fellow – and I'd say a young Orangeman, for we had a genuine all-Ulster listenership – came to Seán with a concertina and a good voice. But the songs he sang could be heard in any dancehall. And it was only after a long talk and almost despair that Seán extracted from him an old song that his granny in the Braid used to sing to the tune of 'The Green Bushes'. The words are worth remembering, if only because they oddly mix up two of the last wars of Empire and also add up to one of the few ballads to mention a factory as a thing of beauty:

> Down among the young laurels of Bonny Wood Green
> Where me and me true-love have oftimes been seen,
> The years have rolled on where so happy were we,
> But 'tis little she thought that a sojer I'd be.
>
> It was early one morn, while the lambs they did play,
> That off to Kells Barracks I straight made my way.
> It was there I enlisted to fight for the Queen
> With this cause to uphold I left Bonny Wood Green.
>
> At Larne Harbour our troop-ships lay waiting to sail,
> While mothers were crying and lovers looked pale.
> We were singing and dancing as the bands they did play,
> But 'twas little we thought of our graves faraway.
>
> Oh, in Africa's soil there are diamonds and gold,
> And the scenes of that struggle for wealth, I am told.
> It was there many thousands were doomed to lie low
> In defence of their country while facing the foe.
>
> Far away out in Flanders, at the back of the line,
> We were talking of sweethearts we'd left far behind
> And one Irish soldier says: 'I've got the Queen,
> 'And she works in John Ross's at Bonny Wood Green.'
>
> It was early next morning while charging the foe,
> A shot from the enemy, he was laid low.
> He called to a comrade, a sorrowful scene,
> His thoughts were on Nelly and Bonny Wood Green.
>
> If ever to Ireland you chance for to stray,
> There's a neat little factory near Ballymachveigh,
> Where the weavers and winders are plain to be seen,
> For they all wear white aprons in Bonny Wood Green.

It's a poor programme that can't produce one masterpiece. And that picture of an Ulster bleaching green is, for me, as brightly enamelled as anything in Chaucer's *Parlement of Foules*. And *The Nine Countries of Ulster* also gave me my first experience of reader or listener co-operation. Even to the extent of a group of Orange people from Larne, encountered one night in Galway City during the week of Galway Races. They were singing a drinking song that one of them had written and, out of the blue, or the din, and to my consternation and gratification, one of them called: 'Put that on radio, Ben Kiely.' And I did:

> When I'm old and feeble, and my bones are stiff inset,
> I won't get cross and crankie as some old fogies get.
> For I'm saving every penny to buy a whirly chair
> For to wheel me to the wee room underneath the stair.
> All gay and merry, each in his chair,
> Down in the wee room underneath the stair.

Lost loyal voices singing in Galway at a time when any man was welcome in Larne.

And that programme also gave me the opportunity to meet a rare selection of singers and artists, and to work in great harmony with the Radió Éireann Repertory Company and to treasure up memories of such men as John Stephenson and others of the old stock. And to meet such Ulster people as Honor Edgar and Tom Burns and Jo O'Doherty to mention only three exiled, as I was myself, in Dublin. Years later it had a delightful echo when under the aegis of Ciaran MacMathuna, a quiet, persuasive man, and great scholar in folk music, I found myself in Drumshambo, County Leitrim, adjudicating a ballad-singing contest and, I fear, singing a bit myself. A most memorable occasion.

My own stint, stepping into the shoes of Brinsley MacNamara, came first in the company of the Radió Éireann Singers. The theme for collaboration was *The Songs of Young Ireland* and, as I have said, the series ran for a long time. Yet I do not think that I was stretching the subject too far by looking back from 1848 to 1798, to Drennan who wrote 'The Wake of William Orr', and foward to Francis A. Fahey. For the Young Irelanders, of 1848 and thereabouts, also had their lighter moments. And the tradition in which the men who contributed songs and poems to the *Nation* (1848) did go back to begin with Drennan and forward to end with Fahey. Or not exactly to end.

There was great pleasure in working with the Radió Éireann Singers – a pleasant group of young people, male and female, especially the female – and in observing the relationship between the group and their German conductor, Dr Hans Waldemar Rosen: nieces and nephews gathered around a fussy and eccentric, but kindly, uncle. There were moments of high amusement both in Henry Street and in a strange recording studio by Portobello Bridge in the south city.

Once, I recall, I had written a script that was nothing if not patriotic and that included the Aubrey de Vere poem: 'On the green hills of Ulster the white cross waves high.' And goes on to proclaim: 'Our trust is in God and in Rory O'More.' Meaning Rory, the great chieftain, warring against the English. But through a hiatus in communications the song that came up at rehearsal was Samuel Lover's light and lilting piece about young Rory O'More, the good-hearted peasant, loving Kathleen Bawn – or something of that sort. Right up to that moment of truth I had a suspicion that the soloist, Joe McNally, was smiling at some secret joke; which, he afterwards confessed to me, was the truth. He was waiting to see the faces of Dr Rosen and myself when we realised we were in the middle of a minor comedy of errors. An even more humorous man, the actor, Seamus Kavanagh, said afterwards that we were lucky we didn't come up with the epic of Brian O'Lynn who wore his breeches inside out:

> Brian O'Lynn had no breeches to wear,
> So he bought an old sheepskin to make him a pair.
> 'With the glossy side out and the hairy side in,
> They'll tickle me fancy,' said Brian O'Lynn.

But what was to be done? We were going on the air, live, in a few hours. No easy recording sessions in those days. Nothing for it but to alter the script. Which I did. And in place of his namesake, the great chieftain, the young peasant Rory O'More marched off with the most perfervid of the patriots. Which would have surprised even Samuel Lover, that princely Dublin jack of all trades.

That *Young Ireland* series did not surpass Brinsley's time-enduring record with the melodies of Thomas Moore any more than my later *Nine Counties of Ulster* did. But due to an expansive interpretation of history, it did last for more than a year. And Colm O'Lochlainn was again, as in all matters of the sort, of the utmost assistance in finding the right melodies for old songs. For, as I have mentioned, it was he who told me that James Clarence Mangan's song 'Oh, Woman of Three Cows', translated from the Irish, went to the music of 'Ghost Riders in the Sky'.

Two other programmes brought me into even closer and always rewarding association with Francis MacManus. One of them consisted of dramatised selections from the Irish novelists of the nineteenth century and it was called *Between the Fire and the Wall*. That title was borrowed from the beginning of a poem by Austin Clarke:

> Oh, storyteller, do not tire
> Between the fire and the wall. . . .

The programme gave me a rare chance to do some stocktaking in my knowledge of the novels of the period. W. B. Yeats had written a dedication to a book of stories selected from those same novels, and his dedicatory poem, in its earlier and later versions, provided resonant quotations. His selection was 'The Green Branch', hung with many a bell:

> Gay bells or sad, they bring you memories
> Of half-forgotten, innocent old places. . . .
> We and our bitterness have left no traces
> On Munster grass and Connemara skies.

Pollution, though, may change all that. Anyway, it's a good thought for the times we live in. And that programme meant that I was again in contact with the Radió Éireann Repertory, and was confirming friendships that have, I hope, lasted to this day and that now evoke happy and melancholy memories of those who are no longer with us. But there was one programme that was designed to last and didn't. Not through any fault of the basic idea or material, but because the chairman, now deceased – and a very decent man he was – came on the air one evening after a heavy, and unavoidable, dinner party in the Shelbourne Hotel.

For the course of its brief and hapless life that programme was called *Bookman's Round Table*. The idea was that two people, who were supposed to be literary, discussed an author. And the chairman did whatever a chairman is supposed to do in such circumstances.

All life in Ireland, as the dear lady I knew well and highly respected, used to say was a supposition. Everybody was supposed to be doing something else.

Anyway: the first programme in that series went off well. A gentleman whose name was to become so high on television and radio that I'd be too humble to mention it, had the goodness to talk with me about the works of Evelyn Waugh. And the decent and capable chairman had not just previously been to a dinner party. The following week the subject was Canon Sheehan and the authorities were myself and Thomas Hogan, a scholar and an old college contemporary. And the chairman, post prandial, began by saying that he knew damn all about Canon Sheehan but that the plain people of Ireland (he was not Brian O'Nolan who used to write a lot about the plain people if they cared to listen) could hear all about Canon Sheehan from his (the chairman's) learned friends, Thomas Hogan and Benedict Kiely.

Then he left the mike, and that particular glass box, and went off somewhere and I had to go out and bring him back. While Thomas Hogan, as good as any three men, carried on the discussion on his own. That happened several times in the course of the programme. And as far away as Omagh, my home town, the whole thing was accepted as a funny programme. For on that night my mother's wireless had gone dumb and she went to a neighbour's house to listen to her baby boy. On one of the few occasions when the chairman was next or near the mike his contribution was to ask me would I have a cigarette. I said no, I didn't smoke. Which was true. And far away in Omagh the neighbour's daughter said to my venerable parent: 'There you are, Mrs Kiely. He won't smoke. He knows you're listening.'

Afterwards, of course, there had to be an inquiry, and the programme was discontinued, although Frank MacManus said he might keep it on under the title of *Bookmen Under the Table*.

These and other memories, warm and comic and melancholy, were in my mind when, for the last time, I walked, with the members of the *Morning Miscellany* programme, down that longest corridor that I had ever seen, just before broadcasting was transferred south beyond the Dodder. We had, I think, the sad distinction of being the last programme to be broadcast from Henry Street. We left behind us dead, empty rooms, workmen already knocking down partitioning walls and refitting that isle that used to be full of noises (sounds etc. that give delight and hurt not) for other purposes. The ghosts, I supposed, would also have to go. Yet I have not despaired of meeting some of them nowadays, when I slip in at the back of Donnybrook church and walk along a garden path to the new studios. That garden may have its own ghosts but they are not for me. And I think of, among others, Philip Rooney and Brinsley MacNamara, and Denis Meehan and Francis MacManus, and H. L. Morrow and T. J. Kiernan and Seamus Kavanagh and his definitions:

'A Dublinman is a man who doesn't go home for Christmas: he is at home.'

'Incest is cashing a cheque in your own bank.'

And many others.

And I remember Nuala and Donagh MacDonagh, and Delia Murphy and the programme *Ireland is Singing*. And Aunt Kate Gormley and the man who broke out of Omagh jail.

To all of them I owe something. To the shade of Larry Morrow I even owe a whole novel. For once upon a raw and gusty day Larry (H. L.) went around asking people who were supposed to be able to write to, for God's sake, write him plays he could produce on radio: and offering a fair sum of money for a tolerable effort. Tempted by the money I rooted among my notes and came up with six pages I had written down one morning after a remembered dream.

Samuel Taylor Coleridge, do you hear me?

After fierce efforts I gave up trying to write a play: playwriting being an art about which I knew, and know, nothing. And the six pages became a novel called *Honey Seems Bitter*. Out of which (although it was promptly banned, as everything was in Ireland in those days by the Censorship of Publications for being, 'in general tendency indecent or obscene') I did better than I had done out of any novel up to that moment.

Men are we and must weep. The Post Office is now simply a post office, and although that in itself is a good and useful thing, it has no longer got that extra dimension. And although Donnybrook is very fine, and I live there with some contentment, it is not the same thing as Moore Street and the fruit markets and the heart of Old Dublin.

The new studios are splendid, and by the time lichen, if it is permitted, gathers on the walls they will add up even to a more varied and exciting place than they do at present.

And will be something to be written about after another seventy years.

SEVEN

As Well as the Old Bog Road

The year was 1939. Autumn. Although that good Americanism, the Fall, would have been much more apt as a description of that autumn. A war, as most of us had heard, had broken out over by Danzig, now Gdansk. The fall, indeed. Or the marks that we were once told and some of us even believed, the Fall left for the misery of man.

It was in Dublin, on a sleepy Sunday afternoon in north Dublin City, in Hollybrook Road, Clontarf. But in the house of Brian O'Higgins, Brian na Banban, an ageing and sea-green-incorruptible Irish patriot, there was a very pleasant party going on. Jimmy Broe was on his feet and singing, in one of the best tenor voices I've ever heard, about dreaming of Jeannie with the light brown hair. That voice is long silent. Jimmy died young. He was the son of Treasa Ní Chormaic, the harpist, with whom and with Dennis Cox, the baritone, I had once travelled on the boat from Glasgow to Belfast.

That trip was made in the March of 1946, and I had been to Glasgow, to the Central Hotel in Sauchiehall Street, to give a seasonal talk on the origins, implications, evils etc., etc. of the Partition of Ireland, to the Glasgow–Irish National Association, then well run by a Donegal-born Glaswegian, a good man called, like Brigid whom Bob Williamson married, McGinn. It's a long time, God be thanked, since anybody asked the like of me to give a talk on the origins, or anything else, of the Partition of Ireland.

The harpist and the baritone were coming from an Irish concert in Greenock. They were good company. When I told Dennis Cox that one of my mother's favourite songs ever since she learned it, in Drumquin, County Tyrone, from a Presbyterian lady called Woods, was a song he had recorded for Parlophone Red Label, he up and sang on that boat for the edification of all classes and creeds:

> Erin shall surely awaken
> Out of the depths of despair,
> Glowing her cheeks, Death's empire
> Was never planted there. . . .

That was a long time ago and I am quoting from memory:

> Ireland is Ireland through joy and through tears,
> Hope never dies through the long weary years. . . .

And much and more of the same. And we need all the Hope we can hobble on with.

But back for the moment to the hospitable house of Brian na Banban on Hollybrook Road, Clontarf, and Jimmy Broe, also up and singing, but about Stephen Foster's Jeannie and her light brown hair. While in one corner of the room, where I am sitting half-concealed behind a row of guests, I am listening to the singer but also flicking through a book of comic verse by J. B. Morton. First of all his piece in solemn honour of William Blake:

> I saw a lamb upon a tree
> I stared at it / It stared at me.
> And there all day
> The lamb and I
> Just stared and stared,
> I wonder why!
> I do not know
> Nor does the lamb,
> And neither of us
> Cares a damn.

Then followed something that may have been the love song of a female rhinoceros, or hippopotamus. There was a passage in it that went something like this:

A boom, a crash, a cry of pain, an oath,
My love comes crashing through the undergrowth.

At that exact moment Jimmy was singing that Jeannie's light brown hair was floating like a vapour on the soft summer air: and because of the contrast, and most regrettably, I guffawed. Afterwards I apologised to the singer and to the small, silver-haired lady who was, at that unfortunate moment, seated beside me.

Jimmy forgave me. The lady said that she had at that moment been reading over my shoulder and had noticed the ludicrousity, but that my guffaw had drowned her giggle. On the strength of that silly moment we became friends and she invited me to come some evening to where she lived in Cadogan Road in Fairview, a few steps from Annesley Bridge and the sluggish, muddy, salty, etc., etc. dribble of the Tolka. If it wasn't Cadogan Road it was the one that runs parallel to it.

To meet some friends of hers, she said. She was the poetess Teresa Brayton. The friends turned out to be William Walsh, down from Croydon Park in Marino and bringing his son, Paddy, still my friend, with him. But William was originally of Fore, in the County Westmeath, and was the elder brother of Michael Walsh, the poet of that enchanted place. Not too long after that William introduced me to George Campbell, the painter, then moving from Belfast to Dublin, and to his wife, Madge. But that's another story.

But it was only much later that all of that came back to me when a man I know said to me: 'Did she ever write anything? I mean as well as "The Old Bog Road".' And another man I know, who was visiting a certain provincial public library, found some of the staff searching the half-inch map to find that bog and that road. He had no trouble at all in pointing it out to them or, at any rate, in indicating its location. Upon which one of them said: 'I suppose Percy French would, in the course of his official duties, have been in that part of the country.'

So my man thundered a bit and asked them what Percy French had to do with the case, and enlightened them still further: and his experience drove me to write down somewhat of what I remembered of that silver-haired lady who smiled so pleasantly when I guffawed at the conjunction of the diaphonous hair of Jeannie with J. B. Morton's love song of the hippo, or the rhino, or whatever.

She did write more songs and poems than the one by which she is now mostly remembered in one public library.

There are two books here to my hand: *Songs of the Dawn* and *The Flame of Ireland*, published in New York in 1913 and 1926 respectively: two solid, well-bound books, two hundred-plus pages in all, the first book with a frontispiece photograph of the pretty young woman Teresa was, eighty-six years ago.

How well the books circulated here in Ireland I do not know. But I have been told, and it seems easy to believe it, that there were copies of them in damned near every Irish–American household. These two books were given to me by my friend, the late Kevin Sullivan, when once long ago I told him that I had actually known Teresa.

So I open the pages that on Manhattan Island helped to bring Ireland to a houseful of Sullivans. She wrote in dedication:

> Unto my own, the Irish, I send with smiles and tears
> This little book of melodies caught from the flying years,
> With all the love within me, and with all the best I know,
> I'd call them back o'er many a track to lands of long ago.

She spoke to all of us the Irish, Here and Over There, and to every Irish county. But her preference was, naturally, for Kildare and the eastern Midlands, for Tara and the Stone of Destiny, and for the hallowed grave of the massacred Croppies. She remembered those melancholy grasslands when she herself was in all the loneliness of exile, and in days when the transatlantic journey could sometimes take a fortnight or more: and when, anyway, the exile might never be able to add up the money for the return fare, either for a holiday or for keeps. The lonely mother at home had not become the figure of fun that she later seemed to be to some most insensitive satirists:

> When shadows lie on the lonesome floor
> And night winds stir in the big ash tree,
> Then I sit by myself at the open door
> And cry for the children that's gone from me.

She rose to her best, though, in less melancholy pieces that could be, and were, recited at Irish–American gatherings:

> By the crossroads of Knockallen, where the bog and upland meet
> There's a tidy row of houses that the neighbours call the street.

It is free and independent though it pays its tax to George,
For it runs its own Home Parliament in Jerry Connor's forge.

Or:

'Tis Bonfire Night in Ireland, God, but the years go fast.
And here's myself, a lonesome man who lives but in the past.
The long day's work is over and stars come out above,
But, sure, they're not the stars of home, the ones I used to love.
And neither is this burning night like that old night in June
When Tommy Casey whistled up the Rising of the Moon.

That lonesome man will reappear in her greatest song. You'll find his
brother in Brian Moore's novel *An Answer From Limbo*. Meanwhile
she displayed her loyalty to the land that had adopted her and gave
her, for a time, security and happiness, even if, as I always suspected,
there had been some tragedy in her personal life. There were times
when she could be fey and withdrawn.

She celebrated the rank and file who had died for, as she put it, the
Glory of Columbia, in the American Civil War. For Independence
Day she wrote a thundering piece, quite as rousing as anything in that
class. The verses in the second book, *The Flame of Ireland*, collected
in 1926, were, some of them, written in brooding agony, over death
and civil war, and the Dublin executions, and the murder of Roger
Casement, and all the other things Irish people had to brood about in
the twenties.

One theme remained constant: the desire to return to Ireland:

But I'll go back to Ireland, in life or death I'll go,
For there my soul is waiting with all the loves I know
By windy dawns 'tis waiting, and twilight grey with rain,
And I must go to Ireland to find that soul again.

She put all that at her best in the short poem that begins:

I would know it in the darkness were I deaf and dumb and blind,
I would know it o'er the thrashing of a million miles of foam,
I would know it sun or shadow, I would know it rain or wind,
The road that leads to Ireland, aye, the old road home.

When I met her for the second time the old road home had, as I said,
brought her as far as a bedsitter in Cadogan Road by the Tolka. Later

she left Dublin and went back to Kildare to live with relatives in a roadside cottage near Enfield. Her gift for me on the day of her departure from Dublin was a copy of *St Patrick, the Travelling Man* by Winifred M. Letts: not really a gift for me but for my mother, whom she never met nor ever was to meet.

That roadside cottage was, as I remember it, a rose-embowered place. Or perhaps it was her living presence that made it seem so. William Walsh and his son Paddy, and Brian O'Higgins, Jr., then just making his mark in the Abbey Theatre, used to cycle down to see her: happy journeys to enchanted evenings of talk on nothing stronger than strong tea. When the weather was in it the walking of the Old Bog Road, quite close to the house, was a ceremonial matter.

Once when I walked alone with her, she showed me a dropping, blossoming tree, in the corner of a field and to the left-hand side of the main road as you go west, under which tree she had once seen her long dead sister. No disbelief did I feel. She read Swedenborg very seriously, as was the fashion of her time, but she needed no help from any mystic to repeople her own fields with beloved shadows from the past.

That cottage is long gone now, nor, often as I've passed that way, can I locate the haunted tree. Perhaps the road widening claimed it and claimed also the shadow which, in her vision, it had sheltered.

Because of the persistent mentioning of her name in a column, signed Patrick Lagan and appearing in the *Irish Press* in the early 1960s, Sean J. White and myself may have had, I like to think, some small part in the movement that raised a monument over her grave in Cloncurry graveyard: on one of those strange, little, tree-topped Midland hillocks. Some years ago I stood by that grave with a poet and novelist, the two combined in one man, who since then, and because of his contacts in the corridors of power, has done much good for his hapless brethern. Together we raised our voice, I almost said sang, in what he called the philosophical verse of 'The Old Bog Road'.

If she were sheltering anywhere under a blossoming, drooping tree, she must have smiled at our well-intentioned cacophany. That poet and a few others, and some philosophers, have frequently told me that it is a verse to be proud of. It is the lonesome man, the lonesome exile, speaking:

> This life's a weary puzzle, past finding out by man.
> I take the day for what it's worth and do the best I can.
> Since no one cares a rush for me, what need to make a moan?
> I go my way and draw my pay and smoke my pipe alone.
> Each human heart must know its grief, though bitter be its load.
> So God be with you, Ireland, and the Old Bog Road.

EIGHT

Beginning to Write

A newspaper which I once regularly read in my feeble efforts to keep up with the times, and for which and for everybody connected with it I had the highest respect, once carried out an interesting experiment in Ulster Geographical Studies by placing the town of Newtownstewart in the Foyle Valley: a place which, as we all know, does not, strictly speaking, exist. Newtownstewart, I said to myself, stands between Bessy Bell and Mary Grey (two mountains) where the river Owenkillew pays tribute to the Strule, to create the Mourne, which flows north to Strabane to accept the tribute of the Finn from Donegal, and then to drift slowly to the sea by an estuary and widening loch called the Foyle: widening all the way except at one significant point. Where you may find Derry City.

To the underprivileged who were reared by the Suir, the Nore, the Barrow, the Whang-Ho or the Amazon, all that may seem the vilest pedantry. But it is not so to me nor to many a decent man. And every year with the coming of Spring I feel I must hoist my sail and go. Or better still, leave it a little later, until the meadow-grass along the Strule Valley is at its best: a time of the year I've always loved and which reminds me of the only man I ever knew who consistently, and for the brief time I knew him, called me Ginger.

There may be something odd about a boy who never has nor can ever manage to keep a nickname. In retrospect the matter worries me a little, for any efforts my schoolfellows ever made to give me a nickname just did not succeed. And, since a nickname is as often a mark of popularity as of contumely, I used to worry a bit about that when I was younger. Not any more.

Redheaded I was once. Not flaming red like a good friend of mine from Kinawley, in the County Fermanagh, who had the reddest head in that, or any other, school. Yet I was still red enough to be called Ginger. But nobody at school ever called me that. Not, God knows, that I wanted them to. For it would have been a low-grade class of a nickname, too obvious to imply that anybody had given much thought to the matter, let alone affection or friendship.

Then, when I was about ten years of age, I was doomed to appear at a parochial concert in the town hall to recite, in all its awesome length, that fine patriotic–historical poem: 'The Man From God Knows Where'. An experience of suspense and agony that marked me for life, as my nearest and dearest will sadly tell you. For an encore (whether the audience asked for it or not) a humorous or, as Myles na gCopaleen would have said, a quasi-humorous piece entitled 'When Father Carved the Duck'.

The item that came before me on the programme of the night's delight was a lady doctor from Derry City singing 'The Merry Merry Pipes of Pan'. Looking back on the business from now I daresay she was a handsome woman and a fine singer. But, as I saw her on that night, she could, in voice and appearance, have been one of the weird sisters. For as soon as she stepped out on the stage I knew that I was next for the high jump. With every trill and flourish, every deep sinking note and every soaring flight, my doom came closer. Even when she had done and the echoes of the 'Pipes of Pan' had faded away I still refused to believe it. Until the Christian Brother in charge, who used strong language because he came from Belfast and had been on the missions in China, gave me a push from behind and said: 'Get on there, you bloody fool.'

So out I stepped or stumbled and began:

> In our townland, on a night of snow,
> Rode a man from God-knows-where,
> None of us bade him stay or go,
> Nor deemed him friend, nor damned him foe.
> But we stabled his big roan mare;
> For in our townland we're decent folk.

And if he didn't speak, why none of us spoke,
And we sat till the fire burned low. . . .

It made such a mark on me, like they used to say about the Sacrament of Confirmation, that I could, to this day, recite to you, if you had time to listen, the entire poem. Although I'm prepared to admit that I can't remember two lines of 'When Father Carved the Duck'.

After that heroic public appearance some of my friends, or it may have been my enemies, made a half-hearted effort to call me The Man From God Knows Where. Which was, anyway, mostly the way I felt and feel about this life and everything in it. But that nickname could not survive. It was too long and too clumsy. So that I was forced to go through life without a nickname. Except that one teacher in secondary school called me, a few times, Benjamino. And a college friend used to call me Benvenuto. And it is possible that, behind my back, other names may have been used by other people.

But, outside school, there was one fellow I met who did call me Ginger: the only man, in truth, who in all my life ever called me Ginger more than once. And the thought of him brings me back to the Strule Valley which, unlike the Foyle Valley, does exist. Being much attached to the past and present of that valley it was only natural that when I first made an effort to write a novel that it should also be an effort to celebrate that valley. It was in the public park on the Camowen River, just before it reaches Omagh, one evening in 1936 that I encountered that young soldier, a pleasant young fellow, who right away and without offence addressed me as Ginger. And, as I have mentioned earlier, I later encountered him under arrest for desertion and I started to write about him in that novel that became a story, 'The King's Shilling'.

Glimpses of the valley the runaway soldier ran along are with me still. Reviewing them is a melancholy pleasure. . . .

Down below at the foot of the long slope was the river valley, the spires of the town rising out of the green trees. Thin brown smoke hung high over the roofs, no wind moving it right or left. Beyond the town the land went up again, bright green of young corn and flax, dark green of potato-fields, up to the high, faded pasture and the brown moor. Two round mountain peaks showed like cocks of hay above the last ridge. . . .

He sat on the heather in a sheltered hollow, ate the parcel of food the fat woman had given him, and waited for the day. It came quickly enough in the high place where he was, more slowly below in the long valley. He saw houses and fields and roads and rivers, dimly at first, then clearly as the mists broke and scattered. The red sun came up slowly, and high in the sweet air the larks were singing mad. The last streamer of white mist rose up from the meadows beside the river, broke and vanished in little white puffs. The wide river came twisting and turning down the valley and a shining metalled road cut straight through the square fields. The valley was new and strange, yet something told him that he had seen that river before, and walked on that road. In a dream, maybe, he had seen the place. It was new and it wasn't new. He was lost.

He went up with the slope of the moor and, as he went, the light of the sun darkened and a shower went past before the wind, hiding the valley under a white mist. He sheltered behind the piled stones that marked the highest point of that rough land, while the wind went rushing past, herding before it the broken and tattered clouds, and the last of the shower went up the valley like the trailing white gown of a girl on her wedding morning. From the top of the cairn he saw white farmhouses and green fields and yellow fields, brown bog, dark woods, blue lakes, great straight roads and little twisted roads, three villages and two big towns. But he had no idea where exactly he was. He saw great mountains on the other side of the valley and great mountains far away, the way the river was flowing. But he had no notion where the Border might be nor which road would lead him to safety. . . .

There: that was a glimpse or two of the original, beloved valley along which I sent my friend, the runaway soldier, running. Where did he finally run to? Did he settle? Is he there still? And alive? Would he hear me if I cried out?

But it was a change of location and scenery to faraway Kerry that was to give me the title, to begin with, of my first published novel: *Land Without Stars*. Take a look at this:

In autumn the red and brown of the mountains and trees colour the cooling air. You can leave Killarney behind you, walk along the road that contains the beauties of Muckross on your right hand. And the moving shoulder of Torc Mountain above you on the left. Up and up until everything touristed and ticketed is below in the deep valley, until you feel the colour of the mountains soaking into your eyes, your hair, the fragile fabric of skin, until the silence of the high places has seeped into your soul. Then, if you are that sort of person, you can sit down and listen, positively listen to the advance of winter over and around the mountains, through the high passes, up the deep glens.

The secret of winter is in these places: the cold, rigid secret withering green growth, stilling the dance and sparkle of lake water, driving colour and laughter from little fields to shelter in lonely farmhouses until the spell lifts and the sun returns. The secret of the winter of the Spirit of Man is there, in some subtle, elusive allegory, drawn in symbols of high hills, cold winds, withering foliage, desolate, swamped fields, lonely homesteads. And in mists that filter down through every deep glen, through Glenflesk and around the ruined castle of Killaha, over the bare slope of Scrahanaveal where a poet was born. And over the flat sea-sand beyond Castlemaine where the poet listened to the thunder of the great wave and knew that he and his people were among the most desolate of all men.

The mists gather and the leaves fall. The last few lingering tourists, as valiant and as melancholy as the last few lingering leaves, circle obediently on the Ring of Kerry, down the Laune to Killorglin, up the steep street, out over level moorland until the great stretch of Dingle Bay is visible from the high road under the shadow of Drung Hill. The iron discipline of the tour may relax, allowing these last valiant trippers to pray in the church that grateful men built in Cahirciveen to thank God for giving them Daniel O'Connell. Also: allowing the trippers to look across at Valentia Island from the harbour on the mainland, or down into the clearwater below the harbour wall at the silver mackerel abandoned, between the boats and the salted, iced, packing cases, to the vicious, crawling crabs.

The poet who was born on the slopes of Scrahanaveal mentioned that island in one of his stiff, melodious lamentations, bewailing the Domhnall MacCarthy More that an English queen had made Earl of Clancare and Baron of Valentia:

Dairinis thiar Iarla níl aici 'en chloinn úir,
I Hamburg, mo chíoch Iarla na seabhach siodach subhach.

Dairinis in the West – it has no lord of the noble race.
Woe is me! In Hamburg is the lord of the gentle, merry heroes.

Only a few of the tourists will be interested in those lines or in the memory of that lamentation. Or interested in knowing that another Gaelic poet of those places stood, the best part of two centuries ago, on the height of Coomakesta Pass to sing a Gaelic salutation for the return of the Liberator to the great house at Derrynane: crying out that the great Daniel O'Connell carried his shield before the broken, tattered, barefooted thousands, describing this new democracy in the terms that poets had reserved for eulogies of the wandering Stuarts, crying out that the Hanoverian crown would go down to the dust. These things are memories moving vaguely in mist, and tourists, as a rule, are sensible people who belong to the sun. . . .

What had happened to me to compel me to that wild change of scenery was that a venerable editor, who was also a Kerryman and a Capuchin friar (a man I often think about and mention), had said to me, coming up to the Christmas of 1944, that I should write for him a long essay about the Munster Gaelic poet: Aodhgadhan Ó Raithile. And that I should go down right away to pursue the ghost of the poet through the mists of the Kerry mountains. Which I did. And called the long essay or study, or whatever, of the poet and his time 'Land Without Stars'. The poet handed me the title when he wrote about the suffering land he lived in:

> *Tír gan tartha gan tairbhe i nEirinn!*
> *Tír gan turadh gan buinne gan reiltean!*

> A land without produce or thing of worth of any kind.
> A land without dry weather, without a stream, without a star!

And since I was then struggling with or brooding over what was to be my first novel I borrowed the title. It seemed most apt: *Land Without Stars*. For I was trying to write about young brooding men in political trouble in the Six Counties that the Partition of Ireland by England (Government of Ireland Act, 1920) had so woefully established as a sort of limbo under the odd and not quite accurate title of Northern Ireland.

My friend, Pat Boyle, a fine novelist and story writer and, also, a bank manager, used to say, in moments of high ridicule, that you could stand in the 1920 Northern Ireland and look due north at Southern Ireland. He meant that you could stand on Macgilligan Strand in County Derry and look up there at Malin Head in County

Donegal: the most northerly tip of the whole holy island of Ireland. Try it on a good day. . . .

There have frequently been young men and others in trouble in the Six Counties since then. We all know that. And my novel was an echo of much that had happened before, and perhaps, a clinking admonition foretelling much that was to come over very long years.

Then in 1946, when the novel was published, a lady reviewer who lived well down into Munster said that it was obvious that the author knew nothing about young people in the North of Ireland. Since at that time one of the few things I knew anything about was young people in the North of Ireland I developed the oddest ideas about lady reviewers. Or just about reviewers, including myself. Now, about fifty years later, I wonder. The young people in the novel seem so innocent. More innocent than I was when I wrote about them.

Was it a more innocent world? Or has the world never been any better or any worse? The young IRA men in the 1930s read *Mein Kampf* because Hitler was against England. But their world was still innocent of the full implications and sideshows of the Hitler war. Of the revelations of Belsen, of Katyn Wood, of Hiroshima, of napalm in Vietnam. Of the Abercorn Restaurant and Derry's Bloody Sunday, of Belfast's Bloody Friday, of the Chicago murders, of Charley Manson and the slaughter of Sharon Tate. The moon was still a virgin, that orbed maiden with white fire laden, and not an ash-heap. Most Irish rivers ran clean. The streets were not constipated with motor cars. Nor did you breathe carbon monoxide on O'Connell Bridge. No, no, nothing worse than the homely body odour of Anna Livia Plurabelle.

In 1973, when I was writing an introduction for a new paperback of *Land Without Stars*, I went on like that and like this:

> *Mein Kampf* by now is somewhat out of fashion and the young IRA men, if they read at all, may read about Cyprus or Algiers, or the hallowed conventionalities of Ché Guevara. Davy Quinn [a character in the novel] already knew about handbooks telling you how to blow things up, but it is doubtful if his feelings on his first visit to Dublin, or his simple romanticism about that city, would now be shared by any young fellows. The proliferation of automobiles, with or without bombs, has made Dublin so much more accessible, and less desirable. It's doubtful, too, if a young man with even a suspicion of Davy's politics or religion, would now get any class of a job in the

Post Office in the Six Counties. Because over the intervening years Stormont managed to tamper with the integrity of that then impeccable British Socialist institution. It was a relative of mine who said, back in those days, that because he was an official in the British Post Office, he was, of necessity, a Socialist. He, also, read Ruskin, Shaw, Wells, Gissing and Emerson and *The Ragged Trousered Philanthropists*.

The town cinema is no longer the social centre it was. It's not even safe. And television is with us. And the Back Alley [a thoroughfare, once, in the home town and in that novel] is no longer with us. And there are new handsome suburbs. But there are bombed and burned-out ruins on the High Street.

Rita Keenan was the young leading lady in that *Land Without Stars*. So, twenty-seven years after I wrote that novel, I had the ill manners to suggest that Rita Keenan's dark skirt would 'nowadays hardly cover her rump, let alone her knees'. Her school of ballroom dancing and the days when people quickstepped to the jingle of hanging out the washing on the Siegfried Line, were worlds away from the leaping, screaming showbands of 1973.

Ancient superstitions lived on into Rita Keenan's world. The girl that drew the clerical student away from his calling would never have luck. That, and many more odd beliefs, had gone on the wind by 1973, and even clerical novitiates, I was told, were not what they had been.

Odd things peep out at me as I reread. Peter and Jacob, two odd old men in the novel, had appeared, more elaborately and more happily in a later short story, 'Homes on the Mountain', and afterwards in the collection, called after another story, 'A Journey to the Seven Streams'. The ill luck or hard fate of Dick Slevin, a lawless young man in *Land Without Stars*, was also that of the eponymous character in a story, 'The Wild Boy', in that same collection. But the moral connotation was completely different. Slevin was conscious that he was just a guy who didn't fit in anywhere, while Davy was even more acutely conscious that he was a soldier of the Irish Republic. They may have had their parallels in the years that followed even if there were only two violent deaths in *Land Without Stars*, a mere preprandial trifle compared with what happened in the 1970s and afterwards. Slevin was also aware that he had blood on his hands and in a row, in the novel, with a stiff-necked ex-celibate or failed clerical student, it was the hunted killer who had the last word. What that was all about I cannot quite remember.

In 1946 that portrait of Dick Slevin drew down on me the disapproval of some young men then rusticating, from crimes of violence, in Crumlin Jail in Belfast. Joseph Tomelty, novelist, playwright, actor, Belfastman, and a dear friend of mine own, had been similarly disapproved of. But the veto of the young men in Crumlin was vetoed by another inmate, Hugh McAteer, and two of those young men, when they were later at large, became firm friends of mine.

It startles me to be reminded by myself how the Big War silenced the church bells. Away back about 1911 Winston Churchill, at whom the Orangemen merrily threw stones in Belfast, made an understandably irritated remark about the dismal spires of Tyrone and Fermanagh. But during the terrible years when he stood up to rescue everybody, the spires were even more dismal because they were dumb, and held in reserve either for calamitous tocsin or final jubilation. It is, perhaps, even more heart-rending to be reminded, as we are from year to year, that parts of the world did not rejoice in peace.

To write a foreword to one's own book was, of course, a sly way of reviewing oneself, twenty-seven years later. Yet the temptation to compare past and present was and is strong, and I suppose that in our accelerated world anything becomes history after twenty-seven years. A description, in the novel, *Land Without Stars*, of my home town on a market day reads now, even to me, like a fragment out of William Carleton and, perhaps, I myself am a figment of Carleton's imagination, or he of mine.

In a later short story, 'Down Then by Derry', an exile returned to his native Ulster town says to some friends: 'When I read the newspapers today there are times I think I was reared in the Garden of Eden.'

And they answer him: 'Weren't we all?'

NINE

Discovering Dublin

The other day, and not so long ago, I went into a pub in the Ballsbridge area of Dublin City with nothing better on my mind than the making of a telephone call. And found myself, as one so often does nowadays, without the necessary open-sesame coinage. So, rattling miscellaneous fragments of metal in my fist, and approaching the counter, I said to the barman, and over the heads of the front-row forwards: 'Would you have two single shillings?'

The conversation along the counter, the rattle of the cash register, even the piped music seemed to die away into silence. And the front-row forwards swivelled round and took a serious look at me.

If, in age, you are over fifty or, still worse, if you are over sixty, or, farandaway worse, if you are over seventy, you may have noticed the number of young people who now infest the pubs and make them quite uninhabitable: no style, no conversation. I wasn't at all like that when I was young. A friend of mine, a notable man in the theatre and on television, said to me one day: 'All the men I once drank with are either cured or dead.' And there are moments when I feel like standing up, with a little help, on a bar stool and proclaiming: 'I drank as a friend, though younger than they were, with R. M. Smyllie, a great editor; and M. J. MacManus, a great literary editor; and Austin Clarke (a most moderate drinker but a very great poet); and Brinsley MacNamara, a great novelist who shook Ireland when he wrote about the Valley of the Squinting Windows ... and with Others, Many

Others. And where did you all, you front-row forwards, holding on to the counter with your elbows as if you owned that counter, where did ye come from all of a sudden?'

But the barman, the other day in Ballsbridge, was a bit older than most of his customers. And he was a sympathetic man. So he said: 'It's a long time now since I heard anyone talking about single shillings.' He spoke like a man remembering the Night of the Big Wind.

'I'll bet,' he said to me, 'if you get on a bus going into Dublin Town, you say the Pillar and never the GPO. Nor *An Lár*. Wherever that may be in this world or the next.'

I admitted that I did, indeed, say or, at any rate, think: The Pillar. Although, as we all know, the Nelson Pillar has been gone these thirty years, or so.

Horatio Nelson stood up there for a long time and was respectfully nodded to by generations of Dublinmen and their ladies, and visitors and ladies, and all. The poet, Louis MacNeice, whom I had the honour of knowing as a friend, walked past there in the darkest days of World War Two and, afterwards, when writing splendidly about Dublin, wrote of 'Nelson on his Pillar, watching his world collapse'. You could, at that time, pay threepence and go up ninety-nine steps and stand at the feet of Nelson and get a fine view of the city: the line of the Liffey there and the blue hills beyond.

Poor Nelson, whose sight was never of the best, hadn't much longer to stand up there to watch anything. Some time in the middle 1960s some imbeciles, or worse, put in a bomb and knocked him off his foothold. Away in Oregon I was at the time, and another fine poet, Robert Farren, wrote to me to comment sadly on the minds, if that would be the word, of the sad cases who could only think of destruction. An army explosives crew had to clean up and remove the remains of the Pillar, a fearful task, one of them told me long afterwards. That Pillar was solidly based. So was the Empire at the time of Trafalgar.

There was a teenage ballroom dance that evening in the Metropole, Dublin, and not at Trafalgar, and many of the young people, including my daughter, Anne, stepped out in the middle of the boom. Mercifully and miraculously nobody was even scratched.

All that, the good man in the pub in Ballsbridge and myself discussed learnedly, rationally and sympathetically. I had admitted that I still might get into a bus and tell the conductor (conductors then still existed) to drop me at the Pillar which no longer existed.

'I do worse,' he said. 'Or better. If I'm getting off at the statue of Daniel O'Connell, which is still there, I say: "Drop me at the Grand Central." ' Which is no longer there.

Then suddenly I saw again the old Grand Central Cinema and even remembered my first visit there. Oh, it was by no means as splendid an occasion as when that precocious boy, or young fellow or changeling, or whatever he was, Marcel Proust (for it is often, if not always, difficult to guess at the age of the Proustian narrator), was brought for the first time to see Therma the Divine on the Parisian stage. 'My pleasure increased further,' Proust remembered, 'when I began to distinguish behind the lowered curtain such obscure noises as one hears through the shell of an egg before the chicken emerges, sounds which presently grew louder, and suddenly, from that world, which, impenetrable to our eyes, yet scrutinised *us* with its own, addressed themselves indubitably to us in the imperious form of three consecutive thumps as thrilling as any signals from the planet Mars.'

No, the Grand Central was not quite on that level. But when my sister, Rita, and her Dublinman of a husband first brought me there, I was young enough, about fourteen, to be so mightily impressed that I still remember the movie. It was called *Five Star Final*, and there was Edward G. Robinson pretending to be the editor of a newspaper in some American city, a sensational newspaper, a sort of a scandal sheet. As so many newspapers nowadays, in a sort of soft-porn way, are. One of the stories that Robinson's paper prints leads to a woman's suicide. And one of the scenes that stays with me to this day showed the woman's daughter rushing into the editor's office and crying out: 'Why did you kill my mother?' And Edward G. Robinson, with a masterly blend of genuine sympathy and fearful irony says: 'We killed your mother for circulation.'

If I cannot remember exactly how long ago that was, I can easily remember that it was in 1932 I paid my first visit to the old Metropole Cinema, now, as all old Dubliners know, no longer there. Gone! In the company of the old Capitol which flourished just around the corner. And the Grand Central had two alcoves, most certainly made for whispering lovers. All gone: along with the palatial Theatre Royal itself and all its most substantial pageants: and leaving not a wrack but a liner-load of memories behind. And all those splendid cinemas and theatres taking with them their fine restaurants and teashops. And what else? Whisper.

But my first visit to the Metropole, in the course of my introduction to Dublin City, is easy to date because it was the Big Sunday of the Eucharistic Congress which Jehovah, or somebody acting in his name, ordained for AD 1932. And never was there, before or since, such a crowd on O'Connell Street. (Although, with tourism and motor traffic nowadays, you never can tell.)

Anyway, my brother, Gerald, and Tom Stanley and my sister, Rita, and myself and a few hundred thousand more, wriggled as best we could across O'Connell Bridge: packed to the parapets because it held, also, the large altar, specially built for the benediction on the great ceremonial Sunday.

Little did I then know (to coin a phrase) that I would spend a year and a half of my life looking at that altar from the balcony of St Joseph's Ward in Cappagh Orthopaedic Hospital. For the great Mother Polycarp, sister to that Dr Cummins who figured so importantly in the life of Sean O'Casey, procured that altar to make a centre for the semicircle of the hospital she was building. Or rather, as she would have put it, Providence procured the altar for her. She had a splendid trust in Providence: God will provide. And, in her case, it would seem that God, or some agent of his, often did.

There was to be a day in Cappagh when Father Joe Furlong was hearing confessions on that balcony. . . .

But I'll hold that story for a while. At the moment I am being introduced to Dublin, and there are five of us fighting our way through thousands, and we're on our way across O'Connell Bridge to see a movie in the Metropole. The things that two single shillings remind you of. Remembrance of things past, how are you? I'm already talking Dublinese.

And the film, or movie, that night in the Metropole was something about crime in New York City, USA. And was called *Two Way Street*. Nothing of it do I remember but the title. Was Jimmy Dunne in it? The actor: not the great Shamrock Rovers footballer of the time. Or Sally Eillers? Have I got her name right? Jimmy, the actor, and Sally, the actress, were a lot together in those days and played together in a movie called *Bad Girl*. And when the bad girl came on the screen and implied that she was expecting (a baby) she electrified Miller's Picture House in my Ulster home town. And on the next Sunday she was mentioned from the pulpit in the Sacred Heart Church.

What, nowadays, could have the same effect? When the Borgias, perhaps, are on the box and the ancient Romans are on the stage in scandals that the ancient Romans were mighty strict about.

I'll say it again: the things that two single shillings remind you of. From Marcel Proust to the first time I saw Jimmy O'Dea as a sort of god, on the Olympia stage, to the last time I talked with him on the window-seat in the old (and now, also, vanished) Red Bank Restaurant in D'Olier Street. And as for all those young people who are allowed into the pubs nowadays, and who have never heard of single shillings, not to mention florins, half-crowns, or thrupenny-bits . . .

Well, we used to say that when you began to notice that Gardai and Christian Brothers looked young, then you, yourself, were growing old. That happened to me a while ago. It was a bit of a shock for me one day when I was reminded that I was older than the Pope.

Which Pope it was I cannot recall.

Also: I hear there are now many new places in Dublin, new places which are much frequented by the front-row forwards.

TEN

Dublin City, There is No Doubtin' . . .

And the best way still to go in search of Dublin City is on foot. Which indicates that the city, although it has, in the more than sixty years during which I have known it, spread and sprawled and not always in an orderly fashion, either in planning or public behaviour, is still handsome and manageable. And the best place to begin that walking tour of Dublin is, perhaps, down by the Liffeyside where the small, now underground, stream, the Poddle, joins Anna Livia Plurabelle and did once form the Black Pool (*Dubh Linn*) that gave the city the name most commonly used.

Southward up the slope, I would suggest, by Winetavern Street which, tradition says, still somewhat follows the curves up which the Norse sea rovers, for security, hauled their boats. Then under the arch of Christchurch Cathedral and down the slope to St Patrick's Cathedral. And in one you may encounter the ghost of Strongbow the Norman. And in the other the ghost of Jonathan Swift:

> The Dean of St Patrick's Cathedral
> Flung open his old-fashioned dures,
> And the ghost of Dean Swift
> Toddled forth in his shift
> To the last of the old-fashioned hures.

Over to the right are the Tailors' Hall and the new and old St Audeon's, and a fragment of the ancient walls of Dublin, and Meath

Street, and the Coombe where you may meet not the ghost but the living presence of Biddy Mulligan, the Pride of the Coombe. She never dies. She lives for ever in the great song by Jimmy O'Dea and Harry O'Donovan:

> You may travel from Clare to the County Kildare,
> From Drogheda down to Macroom,
> But where will you see a fine widow like me,
> Biddy Mulligan the Pride of the Coombe.

Old Dublin is all around you and eternally talkative.

Back then to the centre by way of Dublin Castle, once the centre of British rule in Ireland. Along Dame Street, once much admired by the eminent novelist, Mr Thackeray, as were the dames who then thereon paraded. And on to Trinity College, and Burke and Grattan and Davis. And Goldsmith sipping at the honey pot of his mind. And on to our most tuneful Thomas Moore standing, as Mr Joyce so merrily said, above the Meeting of the Waters – a capacious public urinal.

That for starters. On one walk you may meet twenty people who will recommend other walks, their favourites. So I found it in my early teens when, up from the country, I set out to walk and make my own of Dublin:

> Grey brick upon brick,
> Declamatory bronze
> On sombre pedestals –
> O'Connell, Grattan, Moore –
> And the brewery tugs and the swans
> On the balustraded stream,
> And the bare bones of a fanlight
> Over a hungry door,
> And the air soft on the cheek,
> And porter running from the taps,
> And Nelson on his pillar
> Watching his world collapse.

And that was Louis MacNeice, another Ulsterman and an honoured friend, who loved Dublin well enough to write about it as well or better than anybody else.

A scholarly young prig of a fellow I was when I first did that walk. And I could hear echoing in my ears the resonant words of Francis Bacon, Viscount Verulam and all that:

'Let him (i.e. a young gentleman on his travels) not stay long in one city or town; more or less, as the place deserveth, but not long: nay, when he stayeth in one city or town, let him change his lodging from one end and part of the town to another; which is a great adamant of acquaintance.'

To the first half of that piece of lordly advice, whether by accident, I have paid little attention. Dublin grew around me and, as I have said, and apart from some years here and there in the USA, I became, if not a Dublinman, at any rate a Dubliner. That distinction, as I have mentioned earlier, I first heard made by Seamus Kavanagh, actor and teacher and media man, and wit and humorist, and definite Dublinman.

Kavanagh also argued that the part of Captain Boyle in Sean O'Casey's *Juno and the Paycock* was specially written for him, even if O'Casey, at the time of writing, had neither met nor heard of Kavanagh, who may not then even have been born. 'But look at me,' Kavanagh would say proudly. 'Look at me. Bullet-head and all. God forewarned O'Casey about me.'

Now the very mention of Seamus Kavanagh brings me right up against one of the joys of living in Dublin. As I have found it. Dublin is a theatrical city, and not only in the material that is presented on the stage. No: there is a certain histrionic thing about the genuine Dublinman or woman. To the eyes and ears of a young man up from the country that histrionic capacity was to be encountered, and listened to with delight, in the open-air market in Moore Street on the Northside. Or, and on the south bank of the Liffey, and up the hill, and in the Saturday rush around Thomas Street and High Street and the Coombe in the Liberties, the oldest heart of the Old City. A great city has many hearts.

It may have been just the natural Irish gift of ability in quick conversation. Many peoples have it but in a different way. The softness of the air, which is a polite way of talking about frequent mizzling rain, may have something to do with it:

And the air soft on the cheek. . . .

To that poet who was no Dublinman, and not even a Dubliner, to the poem, and to the sad truth that Nelson is no longer on his pillar, I may return.

But apart from the impromptu theatre of the streets and the public houses, the legitimate theatre, and the social life around it, has always been and continues to be an important part of life in Dublin. Nor do I think that it so seemed to me simply from the happy accident of my having, right from my earliest Dublin days, enjoyed the friendship of men and women of the theatre. Beginning with Brian O'Higgins, of the Abbey, whose father, a renowned and dogged old patriot, and whose mother and sister and brothers I had the happiness of encountering in the late 1930s.

Brian it was who brought me to that most happy social occasion, the party backstage in the Abbey when the beautiful young actress, Eithne Dunne, and the playwright and actor, Gerard Healy, were celebrating the fact that they were to be married the day after.

In the years that followed, as a journalist and even for a period as a theatre critic, I was much in the company of such pleasant people. It is a stiff test for your integrity, and also for your capacity for friendship, to move in a small city among people whose work you may have to evaluate. Did I pass the test? Ask the Shadows. I would not dare to answer.

But don't think for a moment that I ignored the second part of the advice of the eminent Viscount Verulam, Francis Bacon. That bit, I mean, that tells the young gentleman to change his lodging from one end and part of the town to another, and thus to make his acquaintance with the town as adamant and enduring as granite. That I did. Or rather, my way of life just worked out like that.

Before 1940 I had, though, introduced myself to the city which had received me with equanimity. It was a great advantage to have an elder sister settled in the place and married to a Dublinman. So that a few weeks out of my school holidays could be spent in Dublin: first in Amiens Street (Northside) then in Terenure (Southside), and back again across the Liffey to Clonliffe Road, and then to Ballybough.

And since my final settlement in 1940 I have graced five different quarters of the great town: Ballybough, again, and Fairview, neighbours to each other and on the Northside, and Dollymount at the far end of Clontarf and then practically on the northern fringe of the city. Then southwards across the Liffey to elegant Rathgar. And then to Donnybrook where, to the historical imagination, the echoes of the famous, or notorious, Donnybrook Fair can still be heard. It did give a word to the American language.

Through Ballybough and Fairview there stalked, after 1941, the ghost of that young man by the name of Joyce. And he walked before me as I trudged across town to University College, Earlsfort Terrace, Dublin. Where, in the neighbourhood, one might also encounter the ghosts of John Henry Newman and Gerard Manley Hopkins and Thomas MacDonagh. And many others. Over the years the gathering of ghosts continues to grow.

From my study window in Dollymount, I could look down on the Strand and the Bull Island where Joyce sent Stephen Dedalus, created by Joyce in his own image and likeness, walking to see the goddess of a girl wading in the salt water. And I could also look across the Bull Island to Howth Head. And southward across the Bay to the ever-present Dublin and the Wicklow Mountains.

Rathgar Road began the slope that went up to those mountains (hills to you, if you live by the Cascades.) And my next-door neighbour in Rathgar was the scholar and antiquarian, and medical man, Dr George A. Little who made a wonderful book out of the memories of an old mountainy man by the name of Malachi Horan: *Malachi Horan Remembers*.

The hills, in a way, belong to the city. And young Dublin people have always been very conscious of that.

The famous Donnybrook Fair that acquired its charter under that odd fellow, King John, and that lasted well into the nineteenth century, may have gone from Donnybrook. But the place has still preserved many of the good qualities of a good village. In spite of the unending tempest of modern traffic. To step out on the simplest errand may mean a lot of friendly talking with neighbours, young and old. A great time-waster, you may say. But also, it warms the heart.

ELEVEN

As Far as Artane

'The Superior, the Very Reverend John Conmee, SJ, reset his smooth watch in his interior pocket as he came down the presbytery steps. Five to three. Just nice time to walk to Artane. What was that boy's name again? Dignam, yes. Vere dignum et justum est.'

Any copy of *Ulysses* that I have ever possessed always seemed to open naturally at that moment when Father Conmee heads off from the steps of Belvedere College to walk the ways of north Dublin City as far as Artane. But not to walk all the way. No. For Father Conmee disliked to traverse on foot the then-not-so-elegant road that would now be the reach of the North Strand Road to the east of Ballybough and over the River Tolka at Annesley Bridge. In those days, and even in the days of my own first memories of Dublin City, the fine expanses of Fairview Park had not come into existence. And the area between the road and the railway was slobland, and very dirty slob at that.

Away, away back before all that, Ballybough or *Baile na mBocht* (the Place of the Poor), or Mud Island, as it was called by Them that didn't have the Language, had been a sort of robbers' colony with its own king. And the first king had been, like myself, an Ulsterman, one of three brothers who had fled for refuge to Dublin some time about the fall of the Great O'Neill: *See* Joyce: *The Neighbourhood of Dublin*.

So to avoid that then unattractive stretch of road, Father Conmee took the tram at Newcomen Bridge, paid his penny and went as far as the stop at the Howth Road. Then walked on up the Malahide Road, delightfully meditating as he walked:

> The Malahide Road was quiet. It pleased Father Conmee, road and name. The joybells were ringing in gay Malahide. Lord Talbot de Malahide, immediate hereditary lord admiral of Malahide and the seas adjoining.

Meditating on everything from Gerald Griffin's poem on the bridal of Malahide to the doubtful tempers of the old ladies in the home in Portland Row, from the conversion of the heathen, and on the Cockney accent of the fashionable Catholic pulpit-preacher, Father Bernard Vaughan, Father Conmee sails calmly on his way, on a June day, and reads his Holy Office. And sees a flushed-in-the-face young man coming from a gap in the hedge and, following him, a young woman with wild nodding daisies in her hand.

Father Conmee gravely blesses the pair of them and turns a thin page of his breviary. The young man raises his cap. The young woman detaches from her light skirt a clinging twig. It is a movement and a moment of great humour and great beauty. The cloister, even if it were a sort of bourgeois cloister, and the wild earth have met and acknowledged each other.

Joyce knew his Jesuits and his Father Conmee. As the late Kevin Sullivan, an American scholar who was, for a time, an embryo Jesuit, and also a dear friend of mine, emphasised in his valuable study, *Joyce Among the Jesuits*.

Joyce had written:

> Father Conmee, reading his office, watched a flock of muttoning clouds over Rathcoffey. His thin-socked ankles were tickled by the stubble of Clongowes field. He walked there, reading in the evening and heard the cries of the boys' lines at their play, young cries in the quiet evening. He was their rector. His reign was mild.

And the almost six pages of *Ulysses*, the book we have all heard of, in which Conmee, most livingly, appears, add up to one of the many delightful living portraits that all go together to create a whole city, a whole world.

And James Joyce had read Father Conmee's little book of reminiscences, *Old Times in the Barony*. That was a gentle account of languid days in and around the town of Athlone which, in that booklet, was referred to throughout as Luainford. Father Conmee, the real man, wrote: 'There is a valley in the very heart of Ireland that merits more notice and regard than it has been its fate to get from this generation.' He prefaced his sentimental memories with a quotation from John Greenleaf Whittier:

> Sit with me by the homestead hearth
> And stretch the hands of memory forth
> To warm them at the woodfire's blaze.
> And thanks untraced to lips unknown
> Shall greet me like the odours blown
> From unseen meadows newly mown,
> Or lilies floating in some pond,
> Woodfringed, the wayside gaze beyond.
> The traveller knows the grateful sense
> Of sweetness near, he knows not whence,
> And pausing takes, with forehead bare,
> The benediction of the air.

The first place in which I ever saw a copy of Father Conmee's little book was in what was called the *Ad Usum* library in the Jesuit novitiate in Emo Park in the County Laoighis. That was the library in common use by the novices. And since a novitiate is, or was then, supposed to be a house of prayer, secular or profane literature was not lavishly represented there.

But over the years the oddest things had drifted on to those shelves in the highest corridor of that old house. And Bell's *Reciter* and Dr Beecher's *Elocution*, and oddments of that nature, were to be found along with Father Peter Gallwey, SJ, on *The Watches of the Passion*, and Scaramelli on *The Spiritual Life*, and St Alphonsus and St Francis de Sales on *The Love of God*, and Father Faber of the Oratory oozing on forever about *Bethlehem and Calvary*, and Bishop Goodier's *Life of Christ*, and Père Ploo (spelled Plus), a French Jesuit, and the meditation books of Mother Mary Loyola. She was referred to, I regret to say, by a humorous novice from Galway, who afterwards distinguished himself on the missions in Rhodesia as, Mother Mary-Lie-Over.

Even *The Spirit of the Nation* was there: all green except for the golden harps. And one late vocation, with a fine Oxford accent, used to amuse himself and everybody else by walking in the grounds in the early morning at a religious duty known as Voice Production, and reading with great function and in the most ineffable Oxford accent: 'Left Right, Left Right, Steady Boys and Step Together.'

As mentioned earlier, the first man I ever heard praising, or defending, James Joyce was an Irish Christian Brother: and to a class of us (at trigonometry) who had pretty hazy ideas as to what he was getting worked up about. But the first discussion I ever heard on Joyce was there in that novitiate. It centred around whether Joyce had been an OB or an OC. Being an OCB myself and from the wilds of Ulster where Jesuit schools were not exactly tripping over each other, it took me a while to realise that what was meant was Old Belvederian and Old Clongownian.

And up in that high corridor Father Conmee slumbered on a corner of the shelves, remembering Old Times in the Barony, and saying with amiable pomposity: 'What a throng of incidents recall themselves, in which tragedy and comedy, awe and familiarity jostle one another in the highway or the hovel, before the justice seat and even in the house of God! Who will weave them into works of deathless fancy, before they are quite forgotten, and before the passing away of those whose memory is the spell that summons them to life again.'

Well, Mr James Joyce, who was a bit of an OC and a bit of an OB, was to specialise in a big way in that business of weaving memories into deathless fancy. And he was to set Father J. S. Conmee, SJ, walking forever from Gardiner Street to Artane on a June day ninety-five years ago. Here he goes. And as he walks he works out an aristocratic case of conscience:

> At the Howth road stop Father Conmee alighted, was saluted by the conductor and saluted in his turn.
> The Malahide road was quiet. It pleased Father Conmee, road and name. The joybells were ringing in gay Malahide. Lord Talbot de Malahide, immediate hereditary lord admiral of Malahide and the seas adjoining. Then came the call to arms and she was maid, wife and widow in one day. Those were oldwordish days, loyal times in

joyous townlands, old times in the barony.

Father Conmee, walking, thought of his little book *Old Times in the Barony* and of the book that might be written about Jesuit houses and of Mary Rochfort, daughter of lord Molesworth, first countess of Belvedere.

A listless lady, no more young, walked alone the shore of lough Ennel, Mary, first countess of Belvedere, listlessly walking in the evening, not startled when an otter plunged. Who could know the truth? Not the jealous lord Belvedere and not her confessor if she had not committed adultery fully, *eiaculatio seminis inter vas naturale mulieris*, with her husband's brother? She would half confess if she had not all sinned as women did. Only God knew and she and he, her husband's brother.

Father Conmee thought of that tyrannous incontinence, needed however for men's race on earth, and of the ways of God which were not our ways.

TWELVE

The Liberties of Dublin

The first reference that I ever encountered to the Liberties of Dublin was, I suspect, in the statement that the young Mr Yeats made in his collection of prose pieces, *The Celtic Twilight*, about Zozimus, the Last of the Gleemen. That may seem to imply that myself and the other gentle scholars attending the Christian Brothers' School at Mount St Columba in Omagh, County Tyrone, never had the noses out of the best books. Nor had any interest at all in screen magazines with pictures of Ginger Rogers and others: very demure pictures compared with the honest presentations of the present. It may even seem to imply that from an early age we had been familiar with the prose of our greatest poet.

The truth is more simple. That essay was included in an Everyman anthology that we used, or had to use, as a text in secondary school. Some survivors may still remember that at school in those days you had the essay form for breakfast, dinner, tea and supper, almost as if no other literary form existed. And as if there was no future for us except to spend our days trying to write like Addison, Steele, Lamb, Hazlitt, E. V. Lucas, Robert Lynd, A. A. Milne, Chesterton, Belloc, or A. G. Gardiner of *The Daily News*, who quaintly called himself 'Alpha of the Plough'.

I don't go to school any more. So I don't know what it's like nowadays. But I am told that novels and short stories are not unheard of and that it is even admitted that Irish writers, not yet dead, may be read with impunity.

From that tribute to one poet, Zozimus, by another poet, Mr Yeats, names like Black Pitts and Faddle Alley leaped into the imagination and stayed there for ever. So that when I read once in the newspapers that a committee up in the Liberties was leading the relevant government minister around the ancient streets to convince him that the Liberties should be preserved, the first words I said to myself were 'Black Pitts' and 'Faddle Alley'.

Neither the minister nor anybody else should have needed much persuading. The great buildings, mostly churches, will, as we all know or hope, stand as long as the city stands: Christchurch, St Patrick's, John's Lane *et alibi, aliorum.* . . . The great names will, we hope, be remembered as long as we have a memory. But there was more to it than that. The Liberties were – and although depleted and diminished by bad planning or no planning at all, still are – a special sort of place: the germ and origin of the whole democratic city, a distinct community with its own traditions and pride and associations and closely knit relationships: an example, indeed, of what a real living community should be. As a member of the Liberties Committee once said on a television discussion: 'No society can afford to lose this kind of community.'

Of course, every considerable town in Ireland has its Liberties, or a vestige of something like them. Irishtown, in my own town of Omagh, even has its historic monument: the old humpy bridge over the Drumragh, or Owenreagh River. It is commonly called the Crevnagh Bridge but it is also known as the King's Bridge. There's a tradition, a good story but very vague, that James Stuart sat on his horse on that bridge and watched Omagh burn behind him as the Jacobites fell back from the walls of Derry.

But apart from the King's Bridge, Irishtown, Omagh, is just a few houses and the gasworks. Nor could anybody claim that it has its own distinctive way of life. But the Liberties of Dublin is, or are, a world apart.

This dawned on me first many years ago, about the time when the first scatterment of the Liberties to the new suburbs began. One day, in a pub in the Coombe, I sat with an old man who came back every day to his native place to meet old friends and to drink, slowly and sadly, his one pint. No exile of Erin coming to the beach, in what they used to call the New World, to look homeward over the cold, tempestuous, dividing ocean could more sharply have touched the heart.

When I asked him where he now lived he waved his hand vaguely and said: 'Out there. Out there. Halfways to bloody Limerick.'

Then one night I was up in Francis Street with two friends in a fine restaurant called the Old Dublin. What else could it possibly be called? One of the friends whom we will call Sean, for such, indeed, was his name, was Irish. But back on a brief holiday from his office on Fifth Avenue, Manhattan Island. And wearing one of those flowing ties that, after fifteen or sixteen years of banishment, had just then swept back into fashion. The other friend, whom we will call Kevin, was born and bred on that same Manhattan Island.

Filled with fine fat duck and rich red wine we are burping our way homeward along Francis Street when Sean, who has a sharp eye for such things, sees through a pub window a set of those old-fashioned hanging scales, the ones that pull down and snap up and were a great rarity even in those days. We also hear the singing. So in we go to a night of such fun and good company as was really memorable.

Said Kevin: 'Why didn't you bring me here before? This isn't Dublin at all.'

He was wrong, of course. It was Dublin before what he knew as Dublin existed.

One great friend we made in that pub, a man I'd met in such faraway foreign parts as Eden Quay. Although he did not remember meeting me. Late in the night he looked seriously at Sean's necktie and said: 'Where do you come from?'

'Ireland,' Sean admitted.

That didn't make much impression.

'Manhattan,' said Kevin.

'God pity you,' said our friend. 'You're a poor exile.'

'But as for you,' he said to me. 'Your speech doth bewray you.'

It was no use in the world to tell him I had lived in Dublin for thirty years. He said, sympathetically, that it must have been the suburbs. He asked me where. To say Dollymount (and no harm to it) would have been to invite a snigger. To say Rathgar might have got me thrown out. So I chose respectability and said: 'Ballybough and

Fairview.' Having lived, as I said, in my itinerant career in all four places.

'Dublin was Dublin,' he said, 'when Ballybough was bona fide.'

No use in the world to tell him that Ballybough, once upon a time, had had its own king.

'King of Mud Island,' he said. 'And that was a den of robbers. And what's more, the first king and his two brothers come from the North of Ireland.'

The sons of the Liberties know their history. They should. They were there before any of us were heard of.

And one evening in the 1950s a quiet American came, looking for me, into Michael O'Connell's pub, The White Horse, as then was on Burgh Quay in the centre of the City of Dublin. Because somebody had told him that he might find me there. That was not to suggest that I then lived in that happy house. By no means.

But it happened to be next door to the office in which I, and many others, went through the motions of producing a newspaper: the *Irish Press*. Now, alas, no longer with us, and not through any fault of ours.

In lulls in this great work of informing and educating our fellow countrymen by giving them nothing less than the Truth in the News it was not unheard of that some of us would cool our fevered brows in the White Horse. The others could be at similar cooling operations in other resthouses in the vicinity. Some even crossed the Liffey, with the help of Butt Bridge, as far as Barney's, or the Abbey Bar and Tommy Lennon. But they were restless and adventurous men and were already halfways to Fleet Street, London. As it was then.

This quiet and serious American did, to give him his due, look for me first at the office. But, not finding me there, he went farther and fared worse. Because what he wanted me for was a serious talk about writing in Ireland. And while the White Horse had many advantages, suitability for academic seminars was not one of them. It was a good season, too, for everything but quiet talks. A lot of people seemed to be getting married. A lot of newspapermen seemed to be changing jobs. This could have meant no more than crossing the street from one office to another. But any excuse was good enough for a celebration. And when one man wasn't singing about 'Adieu to Belashanny' and 'The Winding Banks of Erne', or 'The Valley of

Knockanure', another might be remembering 'The Galway Shawl' or 'Your Own Father's Garden in the County Tyrone'. Or 'The Sash' itself. That season, indeed, 'The Sash' was a neighbourly sort of a joke.

You know: it occurred to me then that in spite of the torrents of talk in the Dublin pubs, it was doubtful if anybody much went to a pub in our day hellbent on emulating Samuel Johnson or Edmund Burke. Company was the need. And drink, in that order. Except you were a very bad case and went primarily for the drink. Song might arise if the need for song arose. And it was this quiet American's misfortune that not knowing our Irish way of life, such as it was or may still be, he always got to the pub when the singing had commenced and the philosophy was over for the night.

He would buy his own glass of stout and sit in and join the company and make a quite futile, because largely unheard, effort to talk sense. Buying your own glass of stout, as most of us used to know, is not the way to ingratiate yourself in an Irish pub. It was not that my American man was mean. It was just that he was not aware of the custom of the country. And how lucky he was. With the price of the stuff, the way it was even then, it was high time for the custom of everybody buying like crazy to come to an end.

For the treating system as we knew it was a curious mixture of generosity and showmanship and downright meanness. We bought rounds either because we felt generous or because we did not want to feel, nor be regarded as, mean. We waited until the other rounds were bought so as to get our own back. And, as a result, every man drank ten times as much as he would have, or should or could have had.

My quiet American wasn't really interested in pubs. It was just that he had heard that Irish people talked in them. He was a modest man. He was quite amazed and grateful when he discovered that I knew who he was. But I knew him as a man who, by the late forties, had written four fine novels. And who had appeared at length in *Spearhead*, a huge anthology of avant-garde literature. Then after the novels he faded out and was mostly forgotten. That can happen at times even to the best writers. Scott Fitzgerald's daughter once told me that her father might have lived longer if, in the years of neglect, he could only have seen a paperback of one of his books in a drugstore.

At any rate: our quiet American passed through the White Horse, went on his way, and was forgotten there as he may have been in other places. And it wasn't until the autumn of 1964, and in a women's college in the State of Virginia, USA, that I again heard his name mentioned. That college awarded annually a prize, one among several, the Nancy Thorpe poetry prize, to one of its students. Nancy Thorpe had been a student there, a brilliant young woman who was killed in a car crash. And her parents in her memory endowed the prize in perpetuity: a noble idea made more noble because of tragedy. Any woman student at any high school east of the Mississippi was eligible. They had to fix some limit but that was still a lot of high schools.

In 1964 the winner was a young lady from New York City. She was a good young poetess and very pleasant to look at, and I was on the committee that made the award. And when I was introduced to the triumphant awardee she smiled most charmingly and said: 'My uncle, Paul Goodman, met you in the White Horse in Dublin.'

Seldom have I come closer to blushing: remembering the din, and the singing of 'The Valley of Knockanure', and 'Your Own Father's Garden in the County Tyrone'. That latter ballad used to be splendidly rendered by a fellow Ulsterman, a journalist who thought better of it, journalism, not the ballad, and went off to prosper in Edinburgh in the antique furniture trade. And in the middle of the savage frivolity of the Irish there was a decent man, with a glass of stout gone flat, and he trying to be serious and, in the end, saying sadly, as he did, that it was no worse than what he had experienced when in the company of Dylan Thomas. The Celts are a hopeless crowd.

But the young and lovely poetess wasn't trying to make ironic comparisons or contrasts. Her uncle had spoken well of us: the singing men of the White Horse. And my interest in him being reawakened, I went to look him up in the college library. For he had resurfaced as a writer. Not this time as a poet, playwright or novelist. All of which he had been. But as a writer of books on the nature of education in our times, and on the problems of the young. With his book, *Growing Up Absurd*, he had made himself a cult figure to

young people feeling the strain of a savagely competitive system that
was the gateway, mostly, to a middle-class life where the pressures
were even more so, and the multiple conformities something that
could not be looked forward to with anything but foreboding. That
book made him not only a messiah to the young but a sort of
precursor for educational reformists of the time to come.

He said that problem children were so because society offered
them only dull jobs and squalid ideals. He said that a modern school
was a teaching machine to train the young by predigested programmes in order to create pre-ordained marketable skills. He wanted
to see the huge modern colleges broken up into small colleges, and
every student choosing his own education: or none at all. He was, of
course, an Utopian. And the logic of his ideas would end up in
everybody mitching, or playing hookey, or going on the gur, as we
used to call that activity in Old Dublin.

Yet which of us could ever say if the compulsory system did not
break as many as it made. And, for myself, I know that I learned more,
reading on my own or fishing in the Drumragh River, than I ever
learned in a class in trigonometry.

It was John Desmond Sheridan, a gentleman and a lively
humorous writer, who made the great joke about trigonometry. He
said that he had spent a lot of time at school learning, by sine and
cosine, how to measure lighthouses. But when he left school he
discovered that all the lighthouses had been measured.

Paul Goodman I met once again when he visited a Southern US
university in which I was going through the motions of teaching. The
White Horse episode he remembered almost with affection. Dublin
had brought us together. And about the time of that latter meeting I
was reading his book, *The Community of Scholars*, in which, with
what he described as conservative anarchy, he was measuring the
weakness of the academic system.

He said: 'People have a right to be crazy, stupid or arrogant. It is
our speciality as human beings. Our mistake is to arm anybody with
collective power. Anarchy is the only safe policy.'

Once again he was being Utopian. And he held that those of us
who are more crazy in the head than are the rest of us, should be
allowed to wander the roads harmlessly as crazy men once did. For

some odd reason, such men, and women, were then called 'fools'. But could our monstrous, high-pressured, mechanical civilisation now find any place for the chastening, sanative nonsense of the Fool in *King Lear*?

In the same issue of *Time* magazine in which I read that Paul Goodman was dead, I read also the fearful story of the sad would-be assassin, Arthur Bremer, the lunatic-at-large in our modern world, the man who shot George Wallace. There he was, wandering about with a gun in his hand, trying to shoot somebody that the world said was important so that he too, Arthur Bremer, could also feel important.

Not too long before he died, Goodman said that he asked only that children should have bright eyes, that the rivers be clean, that food and sex be available, that nobody be pushed around, and that he himself could live on a little. He was sixty and had a heart condition. The years of the 1950s, during which I met him, were, I found, for him years of disillusion and despair. In a play he once wrote about Jonah, the Whaler, he had that misfortunate man saying: 'It should happen to a dog to be a prophet of the Lord of Hosts.'

So he came, I suspect, seeking truth in the White Horse on Burgh (Burra) Quay on the South Bank of Anna Livia Plurabelle, and we gave him only drunken talk and ribald song. Those may have had their own truth.

But then some of us may have seen him merely as a quiet American who wouldn't buy a round.

THIRTEEN

A Meeting with McCormack

In the early 1930s we, that is my schoolfellows and myself, picked up our current and popular music by hanging around bicycle shops. Which also dealt in gramophones. One dear friend of mine who cycled into school from rural parts spent a lot of his time in Peter McAleer's bicycle shop, in the Market Street of Omagh Town, trying to pick up the words and music of Kennedy's 'Red Sails in the Sunset'. He never quite succeeded. Neither with the words nor the music. He died when the minesweeper, on which he was a crew member, was blown up in the Channel in 1941:

> Swift wings we must borrow,
> Make straight for the shore.
> We'll marry tomorrow
> And go sailing no more.

But, anyway, there we were studying music in bicycle shops: We'll build a nest, way up in the West 'neath a sky of heavenly blue. And: A one-room flat and a two-pants suit and three square meals a day. And: I've told every little star just how sweet I think you are; why haven't I told you? And: With a carpet on the floor made of buttercups and clover, all our troubles will be over when we build a little home. . . .

In our more elevated moments we listened to John McCormack and Enrico Caruso and had strong controversy as to which of them was the greater. Caruso had, hadn't he, broken a wineglass just by singing into it? But, then, McCormack was one of our own.

Radio sets were scarce in those days. So were the fourpences for the Pit in the Picture House. And scarcer still was the money to buy the records (discs) we coveted. And not every household had a gramophone. So bicycle shops it had to be. And not until 1977, when I read Gordon T. Ledbetter's fine book, *The Great Irish Tenor*, did I realise why. Not confectioneries nor groceries nor, even, newsagents (wherein you might reasonably expect you could get music with the literature), not drapers, nor haberdashers, nor hardware merchants. No, no. But bicycle shops.

One of the lesser illustrations, in that splendidly illustrated and most knowledgeable book on John McCormack, showed, among other relics of the past, the lid label for an Edison Bell wax cylinder, forerunner of the record and/or the disc. It was dated 1904 and inscribed: 'Songs: Kathleen Mavourneen: McCormack: 6446.' And running around that, yet another inscription: 'John F. Coyne: Cycle Engineer: 115, Dorset Street.'

Gordon T. Ledbetter explained: 'The sale of push-bikes was highly seasonal. So were the sales of phonographs and cylinders. Bicycle sales thrived during the summer and slumped in winter. Phonographs sold well coming up to Christmas and hardly at all after the festive season. Hence the fact that phonographs and cylinders and bicycles were often sold under the one roof in Edwardian days.'

Well, where I came from Edwardian days lasted until 1939. And I hear the oddest stories from other parts of the country.

It may seem that I have laboured long over a small point and one possibly that has long been familiar to many, if not to me. But that was one way of indicating that Ledbetter's fine book was (and remains) not only a brilliant study of John McCormack, man and artist, by an authority who was, as far as was humanly possible, familiar with every note the great singer sang, certainly with every note he recorded, and the way he sang it.

Mr Ledbetter faithfully followed McCormack's career, from the awkward ill-dressed boy, with bad teeth, who emerged from Summerhill College in Sligo and headed for Vincent O'Brien and the *Feis Ceoil*, to the renowned man living like a lord in Moore Abbey, dreaming of Derby winners and being jovial with Edgar Wallace and Beary, the famous jockey.

It was my humble privilege to be in the presence of that great man on a few occasions in his final years. The first encounter was in the offices of the now, alas, long defunct, *Capuchin Annual*, much mentioned by me elsewhere. One of the photographs in Gordon Ledbetter's book came from that publication and showed McCormack in the full regimentals of a Papal Count. The picture was autographed and inscribed: 'God Bless the Capuchin Annual.'

That may sound a little like the inscription allegedly embroidered on an archway in Lower Gardiner Street, Dublin, during the 1932 Eucharistic Congress: 'God Bless Christ the King.' But it did represent the genuine wish of a generous heart. That picture had been part of a valuable symposium feature on McCormack that had appeared in the *Capuchin Annual*.

Remarkable people (as I say elsewhere) passed through the offices of that periodical. And there I met, among others, Maud Gonne, Jack B. Yeats, Thomas MacGreevy (though not for the first time) Michael O'Higgins, T. J. Kiernan, Delia Murphy, Eoin O'Mahoney, *et alibi aliorum, plurimorum sanctorum martyrum et confessorum....*

This is not, believe me, name-dropping. But for a young fellow fresh from the streets and byways of Omagh, the fine county-town of Tyrone, to encounter, all in a lump, such people, such a host of them, was what the Americans might call a Fun Thing.

Another meeting with McCormack is to me for ever memorable. It was in a room above the Dublin pub then known as O'Looney and Rhattigans. A hell of a name. But it was later to be changed in honour of the poet and singer Thomas Moore, who had long ago lived in that house. We were, many of us, in the upstairs lounge bar at a gathering of the Thomas Moore Society while downstairs, in the public bar, the plain men of Dublin drank their black pints with what composure they could muster. So the poet, Patrick Kavanagh, said cheerfully to me. And afterwards wrote.

But upstairs it was Father Senan who suggested that, in honour of Thomas Moore, John McCormack should sing. Thomas Moore would have loved it. With a grace, humility and humour that were, to me, shattering, the great singer stood up to oblige. Just as if you or me were asked, or not asked, to raise our voices in any pub. He began with:

> Love thee dearest, love thee
> Yes, by yonder star I swear. . . .

He went on splendidly and then the voice faltered. There were reasons for that: age and health. Now I happened to have been sitting between McCormack and the great baritone, and most endearing friend, Michael O'Higgins. And when McCormack faltered and stopped he sat down and leaned across me, and said to O'Higgins: 'Michael, pick it up where I left off.'

Which Michael did. And to coin a phrase: There wasn't a dry eye in the room.

Once in New York I told that story to Michael Clarke. Who capped it with one even more moving. His mother and McCormack were great friends, and one day, not too long before the end, mother and son went to visit him. His voice was badly gone. But he sat, with a style and bravery and nobility that Michael found hard to describe, and played some of his recordings, so that, as Mícheál MacLiammóir would have put it, he could still be talking to his friends.

So, he still talks to people all over the world.

Gordon Ledbetter wrote of the singer as storyteller:

> The intimacy with which he sang these songs [i.e. the popular ballads] brought with it the sense that he was confiding in his audience. . . . And few things appeal to human nature so much as being the recipient of confidences. Moreover McCormack seemed to have solved the problem of addressing the subject or object in any particular song at the same time as addressing his audience. There was an apparent ambivalence in his address. His art was the art of reported speech. It was an unusual, almost a unique art. . . .

FOURTEEN

Waiting for the Agent

In that Dublin suburb by the sea where it was elected that I should survive for a while in the 1940s there was, and why should there not have been, a fine public house. For some reason, nor could anybody tell why, it called itself an hotel: the Dollymount Hotel. But it was a splendid public house, not the type of pandemoniacal filling-station, the size of Donnybrook bus garage and every bit as homely and comfortable, that you get nowadays in the new suburbs.

Into that house one day there wandered a nobleman from the other side of the Eastern Sea. He was a stout, tall man with a pale face, pale eyes that didn't look at you, straw-coloured hair and a drooping moustache or Mousie, as it would have been called by the thrawn peasants in the Kincardineshire trilogy of Lewis Grassic Gibbon.

That nobleman was also a dipsomaniac. And no harm to him for that. For most of us are just as far gone and are noisy as well. He was inoffensively quiet. He stayed with us for a long time, three months or more. Yet he was never with us. He lodged somewhere in the neighbourhood. He was on duty punctually every morning when the pub opened. He sat alone at one end of the counter and sipped large brandies. He sipped two bottles of brandy *per diem* and gave offence to nobody. With the coming on of closing time he washed down the brandy with two bottles of Emu Burgundy which came from wherever emus come from, and good luck to men who made it. Then he went home to bed. He seldom staggered.

As he sipped his way through the long arduous day he looked, or stared, steadily at the shelves of bottles behind the bar, and spoke to nobody. And we all, the locals, left him in the peace that he clearly desiderated. That seems a better word, in relation to him, than merely desired. But sometimes he stared at or looked at the advertisements in the newspapers from the auctioneers and the house-property people.

Once I saw him in the centre of Dublin City, in a bank, and I thought, of course, the money has to come from somewhere. The brandy and burgundy, in that suburban pub alone (none of us had ever seen him drinking anywhere else), was then costing him forty-seven pounds a week. Not even a nobleman, perhaps not even a top executive, could afford such money in these more costly days. Unless, that is, he were up to something on the side.

Once, doubting the patents of his nobility, I looked him up in Debrett. I had easy access to Debrett because at that time I worked for my bread in the leader-writers' room of the *Irish Independent*. A Debrett was maintained in that leader-writers' room because that newspaper was (at that time) such a respecter of tradition that right into the 1950s it topped the Social and Personal column every morning with some such throbbing message as: 'Lord Tootmafloot is ninety-two today.'

The leader-writers (four of us) who were supposed to do so, kept forgetting to keep Debrett up to date with the ravages of Death so that quite frequently deceased and long-buried baronets and others found themselves socially and personally celebrating their birthdays.

The editor of that newspaper was a good, honest, considerate man who valued many things that were good: including a papal honour which he was *in plenitudo temporis* to receive. And his friendship with the Earl of Granard. And it would seem that that Earl was one of the many people who consulted that Social and Personal column. So that, quite regularly, the Earl would write to the editor something like this: 'Dear Frank: Happy to see that your paper remembered the birthday of my old friend, Footmagoury of the 42nd Foot. His death six months ago was a severe blow to all his friends.'

The bus that, at that time, brought me to the city from the suburb by the sea deposited me close to Nelson 'on his pillar, watching his world collapse'. And close also to the Abbey Bar, a most happy hostelry, long since absorbed by the tails of the expanding Peacock

Theatre. It was owned and hospitably managed by a man called Tommy Lennon and his gracious lady, Ursula White, who, in her elocution school, taught the art of speech to many young people who afterwards made it notably in the theatre. And that famous Abbey Bar (Mr Yeats' theatre was just round the corner) was frequented by many friends of mine: legal, theatrical, journalistic, God help us. And to brace myself for the deep thought of leader-writing I might have, say, a pincher of Black Bushmills. And one evening one of the legal men said: 'I see in the *Evening Herald* that the Earl of Granard, your editor's friend, is dead.'

Which I announced a little later when I entered the book-lined sanctum of the four leader-writers. As in the case of the evangelists, we were four. And the chief leader-writer, who was also a legal man, stood up and said: 'In God's name, and in the name of Granard who is now near to God, hand me Debrett until I make the excision. We do not wish our editor to receive a letter saying: "Dear Frank, I'm glad to see your paper remembered my birthday. But..."'

It was that same chief legal-leader-writer who, on my first night in that sanctum, said to me: 'You will have two topics. Godless Russia and the Ratepayers' Burden. On any given night, and when requested, you may write three hundred words on any or either of those topics. Give your words any title you please. And, for God's sake, avoid coming to any conclusion about anything.'

But back to where I was a while ago. There in Debrett was my drouthy nobleman, a lot larger than life, generations of him, and wide and windy acres of good English land. A vision I had of coastal erosion, an ocean of brandy and burgundy beating on the shores of the ancestral estates, acre after acre slipping away and sinking into the silent deep. There rolls the deep where grew a tree.

Gradually the news leaked out that the nobleman was there waiting for his agent to catch up with him to purchase a property, house and all, somewhere in rural Ireland. That would explain the interest, if interest it was, and not just something to stare at, instead of the bottles, in the auctioneers' advertisements.

Suppose, I said to myself, the agent never comes. Suppose the nobleman is left sitting here for ever, sipping brandy and washing it down with burgundy, staring at photographs of desirable properties in their own grounds. For ever and ever.

Being, at that time, a young man with literary aspirations, I could see the novel taking shape. I never thought of it as a play, knowing nothing of the theatre. Barring going there for entertainment and being, also and at that time, theatre critic for that newspaper. And afterwards for another, and opposition, newspaper. Also: I knew a lot of actors and actresses, lovely people, particularly the actresses.

But away back at that time in the neighbourhood of Dublin nobody much mentioned Samuel Beckett. Except, say, Con Leventhal of TCD who was his close friend, and Kate O'Brien, Philip Rooney, Tommy Woods (Thomas Hogan), John Jordan, John Montague, Pearse Hutchinson, Tony Cronin and myself, and some others who had all luxuriated in *Murphy*. There were, of course, others again, but I didn't know them at the time. And Eoin O'Brian a great Beckett scholar.

But the two odd fellows who waited for Godot were not, as yet, even there to wait for Godot.

The agent, as it happened, turned up and read the riot act and blamed everybody within sight and hearing for allowing his lord and master to expend that forty-seven pounds a week. But, as we all agreed, it wasn't on us he spent it. And I never did write a novel called *Waiting for the Agent*.

Thirty years later that waiting baronet came back vividly to my memory when I was sitting in the train and on my way to Galway City. Oh, I had remembered him, off and on, over the years. But I had a special reason for remembering him on that journey to Galway. On the way I was to pay my first-ever visit to the Taidhbhearc Theatre, to see a wonderful *Waiting for Godot*, wonderfully performed. And directed by Alan Simpson who was down with me on that train from Dublin. He had already directed his Beckett and his Behan, and many another, in Dublin City.

Alan was a good man to travel with, for he knew the country as only old army men, or ordnance-survey chainmen, could know it: not so much by towns and main roads as by hills, fields, marshes, fences and small streams.

He also knew his Beckett. And was, you might say, the first in the business. And Galway, it had always seemed to me, was the sort of place in which Godot might turn up for the races, for God's sake, and

speaking Irish. Everybody, as the ballad says, was accustomed to turn
up for those ecumenical races:

> There was half a million people there, of all denominations,
> The Catholic, the Protestant, the Jew and Presbyterian.
> There was yet no animosity, no matter what persuasion,
> But *fáilte* and hospitality, inducing fresh acquaintance.

John Butler Yeats, the father of them all, once said that in New York
everything happens: in Dublin nothing happens except the occasional
insolvency. But then, New York is not a city. New York is the whole
world compressed, and everything means everything, good and bad
and in between, and too much of it and all at the same time. Galway
is a small city and a distinct memory of the Middle Ages, and things,
in that ancient city, happen singly and are, more often than not, liable
to be pleasant.

Old Galway friends of mine, some still alive, some gone to God or
Godot, used to keep saying, particularly during Race Week: 'The
place is not what it used to be. You should have been here in the old
days.'

That always set me wondering what they were doing in the old days
that they were not doing all around me at that living and present
moment. There was even the story of the two hearty heroes who
found all the pubs so crowded that they couldn't get a drink in any
comfort. So they bought a barrel, a full one, at a back door, or a half-
barrel or a tierce or half-tierce or whatever, and carted it off to the
bedroom they were sharing in the Southern Hotel.

That was away long ago before the Southern was modernised and
all tarted up, and it had, at that time, a deep stairwell down which you
could look from the topmost floor to the place now, and then, outside
the dining-room. On that space, as our heroes entered, a cocktail
reception was going on. Their room was up at the roof. So they
climbed. And then looked down on the reception. And listened, like
two ancient mariners, to the merry din. And grew dizzy with
temptation, and unstaved one round end of the barrel, and unloaded
the lot, like a tempest, on the well-dressed throng below.

All that was a bit before my time. But I do remember the Pint-
Drinkers' Club in a certain back room. For initiation you had to drink
seventeen pints, one after the other. And then buy a round for

everyone in sight. The rules were framed on the wall. Membership was, naturally, exclusive.

Opening off that back room was a sort of hallway with a blind, ascending stairway. Blind: because it was roofed over to make a larger room above. The great joke was to send a half-tipsy stranger in there, looking for the Gents, and then listen attentively for the thump as he ascended the truncated stairway, on the Road to Nowhere, and his head made contact with the ceiling and he came reeling out again.

Once I was a victim. The echoes of the laughter are with me still. God sees, perhaps I should have been there in the old days.

That back room and the pub before it are long gone. Turned into a shop or something.

But in the train that day, and in the fine company of Alan Simpson, I thought: When the play is over tonight, and whether Godot turns up or not, a party of us will go down the street to the Castle Hotel and talk learnedly for a while. That decision leaves me well content. For I have happy memories of the Castle Hotel, in Lower Abbeygate Street, Galway, which was the true gateway to the Aran Islands.

FIFTEEN

The Corpulent Capuchin and the Flying Curate

Whether we mean it in joy or in sorrow, in peace or in wrath, in kindliness or in utter viciousness, a lot of us have a habit of saying now and again, out aloud so as to be heard, or to our own secret souls: '*Sgríobhfaidh mé leabhar orra*: I'll write a book about them.'

Now: as a man who was a staff journalist for twenty-five years of suffering, and a freelance for as long again, I have a way of saying to myself: 'Editors I have known, I'll write a book about them.'

It could be a long book for I have known a lot of them. But it would by no means be a nasty book, for although editors may have their little human weaknesses, they are not, by no means, among the worst of mankind.

To begin with: I cherish with affection the memory of one editor who sent me off on many a pleasant journey. The first of those journeys was made as far back as 1940: just a little before my twenty-first birthday. I had been absent from my home places for three years and the second half of those three had been spent in an orthopaedic hospital: Cappagh, close to Finglas which was then a village on what were then the northern outskirts of Dublin City. On my way back home through Dublin I called into this editor's office. I had already written something for him. He had paid me well and written me kindly letters. I was anxious to meet him. I was also naturally hoping that he would ask me to write something else for him: and to my great delight and over a cup of tea, he said: 'What would you like to write now?'

Like a child in catechism class I had the answer all ready to reel off, whether I knew what it meant or not. So I said, with all the charming modesty of the young: 'Oh, something like Hilaire Belloc's *The Four Men*. You know: that book he wrote about Sussex. The sort of book that any man would like to write about the county he came from. The sort of book that you would like to write about the Kingdom of Kerry.'

That last sentence was, for me, a clever touch. For that particular editor was a corpulent Kerryman with a beard.

'Done,' he said. 'Write me, not a book now. But five thousand words about your native Tyrone. Set about it how you please. And God go with you. And mind your health. And if you fall into enemy hands up there, give them nothing but your name, rank, and serial number.'

This was the way I set about writing that article. It was to cycle, and I was again back in cycling form, from Maghery where the Ulster Blackwater, sleek, deep and full, flows into Lough Neagh, from Maghery, I repeat, all the way across O'Neill's Tyrone, to my native town of Omagh. No main road did I follow: but zigzagged this way and that, and called in on old friends, and drank tea and ate soda bread in meadows where people were making the hay. No hurry in the world was I in and I had all the time in the world, and the time of my life.

John Hewitt, the poet, whose friendship I was later privileged to have, wrote about his own part of County Armagh, on the southern shore of Lough Neagh, in that same fatal year of 1940:

> Once, walking in the country of my kindred,
> Up the steep hill to where the tower-topped mound
> Still hides their bones, that showery August day,
> I walked right out of Europe into peace.
> For every man I met was relevant. . . .

Well, I cycled mostly and walked a bit and sat around a lot, and it was a lovely way to come home and I owe this joy of that journey, and the memory that still stays with me, to a stout bearded Kerryman, who wore the habit of a Capuchin friar.

Other journeys were to follow. Around Sligo and Leitrim. Once, and all the way, and around the rim of the Nine Counties of Ulster. Then to Killarney and the mountains of Sliabh Luachra to write a long study of Aodhaghan Ó Raithille, the poet. And to Derrynane House to honour the Liberator and see the place transformed into a museum. And to the ruins of Dunboy on Bantry Bay. And all along the route that the great Donal Cam Ó Suilleabháin followed on his fearful wintry march, in the Elizabethan wars, to O'Rourke's place in Leitrim.

In memory I covered all that ground again when, far away in Oregon, I heard of his death and he far away in Australia. He had written to me not long before the end. He had made a long journey from Kerry to find his last resting place.

So I wrote:

> Father Senan Moynihan died in Australia and when a legend dies so far away from its origin and growth there is a danger that it may be o'er-readily forgotten. In the case of Senan, that would be a great pity. It was odd, I remember, to notice how few of the people who should have been there were at the funeral of the poet, Padraic Colum. The weather of that day, I will admit, was one of the worst that ever blew or poured on the side of the Hill of Howth, where the poet was buried. But Padraic had lived to such a fine old age that a lot of people thought he was already dead: and he had lived most of his years elsewhere than Ireland. The legend was lost.

Senan was a corpulent, humorous man and, like the most corpulent of all humorous men, or the most humorous of all corpulent men, he was not only humorous in himself but the cause of humour in others.

So it is only fitting that my memorial to him should begin with a funny story about him. Seán O'Sullivan, the painter, used to refer to him, and to his face and in the most pleasant manner, as Friar Tuck. His very name and something of his warm affability are immortalised in Maurice Walsh's novel, *Blackcock's Feather*. But it was Seán O'Sullivan who twisted a nursery rhyme in his honour. For one of Senan's undeniable gifts was that of making distinguished and influential friends, among them Eleanor Lady Yarrow. And once, when Senan was ill, she brought to visit him Lord Dawson of Penn, physician to the King of England:

All the King's doctors,
And Dawson of Penn,
Came over to put Senan
Together again.

As I think I have said, my own first meeting with Senan was in late 1939. The *Capuchin Annual*, which he edited and created, I had first encountered at the end of 1936 when it was in its eighth year of publication. That would be the issue dated for 1937, a book of about three hundred and thirty pages and not the mammoth of five hundred pages that the *Annual* was later to become, and selling in 1937 for a modest thirty old pence. Today it seems simply unbelievable that so much should have been given away for so little, for next to nothing. I was seventeen years of age at the time and I feel I had only the vaguest idea about the remarkable nature of the publication, from several points of view. Now I look at it with something like awe.

It had retained, and was always to do so, some of the marks of the religious and missionary magazine. After all, it did go out to the world under the banner of a religious and missionary order. So: a Capuchin, Father Fintan, had an article eight pages long, including illustrations, on missionary life: eight pages out of three hundred and thirty. Thereafter the publication took off in a way in which few periodical publications produced by a religious order had ever done before, in Ireland or, insofar as I know, anywhere else.

It is interesting to remember that in 1936–37 you could purchase, among other things, and for half-a-crown, or thirty old pence, nineteen reproductions, eight of them in colour and all of them frameable, of works by Seán O'Sullivan. They are all here in this *Annual*. The frontispiece, indeed, was the painter's imagination of Matt Talbot, the saintly working man of Dublin, on his bended knees. But the long essay that went with it, 'One Man's Years', by the novelist Francis MacManus, was a most unusual piece of hagiography cum social and literary history.

Roibeárd Ó Faracháin's first collection of his poetry had, I was later to find out, made its first (partial, I think) appearance in the issue of the previous year. The 1939 *Annual* carried his poem on the death of G. K. Chesterton: facing that striking photograph of Chesterton reading a book on a bench on the Brighton seafront. And Ó Faracháin also contributed a Thomistic essay, 'God and Man and

Making', on which various people from Eric Gill to Leonard Feeney, SJ, commented. Some gathering! Thomism was the done thing at the time. Yet that essay in aesthetics, like many another feature in the *Annual*, might very well stand up to reprinting.

Then D. L. Kelleher who wrote whimsical glamour books about Ireland and Irish towns, had a set of seventeen simple poems. Michael McLaverty was chief among the contributors of short stories. Gabriel Fallon wrote about the Abbey Theatre. Who knew it better? Séamus MacManus wrote about that golden and eternal old road to Frosses in Donegal, and to the grave of the poetess, his wife, Ethna Carbery.

Then there was that photograph of John McCormack in the full regimentals of a Papal Count, and a gratulatory letter about the *Annual* to Senan from the singer at Moore Abbey on the banks of the Barrow. The *Annual* for 1946–47 was to carry a copious feature, text and photos, on McCormack: one of the features that I specifically mean when I speak of reprinting separately as books.

That photo of and letter from the great singer were only details in that 1937 *Annual*. But I mention them because they remind me that when I came to live permanently in Dublin, and got into the habit of calling in to see Senan, I went in one day to that office in Capel Street to find him with Maud Gonne MacBride, John McCormack, Jack Butler Yeats, Thomas MacCreevy and Michael O'Higgins. Who all seemed to have dropped in casually at about the same time. A scene well set and goodly company. Molly Baxter, Senan's secretary, made the tea: a pleasant, stout, quiet, slow-moving lady who was, possibly, one of the great secretaries of all time, not excluding Machiavelli.

That room in that office at Number Two, Capel Street, on the banks of the Liffey, was an extraordinary place. The office of Capuchin Periodicals then filled the four-storey house except for the ground floor which was occupied by a draper's shop under the reputable name of Lemass. The room where Senan and his Socius, or right-hand man, Father Gerald (frail and saintly and good-humoured and a McGann from Belfast), sat, was up at the top, a combination of office and art gallery, with Jack Yeats and Seán Keating and others on the walls. Those most valuable paintings were, after the passing of Senan, to find other homes.

The office was also, off and on, known as the 'Pope's Boudoir'. Because the famous Eoin – 'Pope' – O'Mahony, rushing hither and yon on one of his many missions of mercy, would sometimes rest for the night in that room on a splendid oaken settle, watched over, as by attendant angels, by the best of contemporary Irish art. The caretaker of the office was a lovely old lady called Annie. For a lot of her life she had worked for a certain Dublin firm that dealt in stationery, mostly envelopes, and she had been paid a lavish ten bob a week. One morning, after something like thirty years' faithful service, she was late for work, and was fined sixpence. When Senan heard that story he offered her the post of chatelaine in Capel Street.

Then on one occasion Eoin O'Mahony, who was down there in Cork where, like many another of the name, he originated, had to journey in a hurry to Dublin and needed accommodation for a night, and sent his telegram: 'Annie, c/o THE CAPUCHIN FATHERS, 2 CAPEL STREET: ARRIVING TO-NIGHT, STOP, LEAVE BEDROOM DOOR OPEN, STOP, POPE.'

Senan had that telegram framed and hung on the wall.

From the comings and goings in that wonderful office it seems logical to proceed to talk of Senan's luncheons and, now and then, dinners, almost invariably in the Clarence or the Gresham Hotels. Some long-nosed, long-faced Malvolios, who were never invited to be there, used to cast eyes up and groan a bit that a member of a mendicant religious order should have an account in class hotels. But apart from the spreading of bonhomie, which should surely be a Franciscan activity, Senan's occasions almost always had, to my memory, some pretty shrewd business purpose connected with the welfare and progress of Capuchin Periodicals: the *Annual*, the quarterly *Bonaventura*, and the monthly, the *Father Mathew Record*.

The guests covered what you might call a wide field: from Paddy the Cope to Frank Sheed, from Peter F. Anson to Séamus MacManus, from Delia Murphy and her songs to Father Terence Connolly, a Jesuit, of Boston, who did a lot of good work on Francis Thompson but who, misfortunately, got up once in the Abbey Theatre to put some theological posers about Mr Yeats' *Purgatory*.

A lot of people assumed that he was a clerical obscurantist and troublemaker when he was only an earnest and typical American student. In his honour and for his benefit I once heard Thomas MacGreevy sing the entire opus of 'The Star-Spangled Banner', and in prime voice, too.

But all this was peripheral to Senan as an encourager of the arts, which indeed he was. He had his weaknesses and his prejudices. To begin with, he was a Kerryman, and Kerrymen have their impulsive and dictatorial twitches. He was very close to Jack B. Yeats and second to none in admiration of his work. But he had a blind spot where The Brother was concerned. As he had also for that most notable of all the editors I have known: R. M. Smyllie. And Senan seemed to regard the Irish Academy of Letters, founded by W. B. Yeats and Bernard Shaw and now extinct, as a sort of subversive organisation which, as a former president, I can assure anybody, it never was. Senan's political vision allowed for only one sun and there were jokes about the number of times that Eamon de Valera's picture appeared in the *Annual*. But Senan did encourage painters, sculptors, musicians and writers with, I think, his judgement, at its best when he was looking at pictures.

He paid well. *Omnibus paribus*, as they seldom are, he had generous ideas on advances and retainers. Often, looking at him, or just meditating on the unusual sort of man he was, I wondered how (although I knew the externals of the story) he had ever found his way into a religious order. For it seemed to me that he would have belonged better as features editor on some big New York magazine. But Time and Place mark all men. Another joke about him was that if he had not become a Capuchin he might, like his Kerry compatriot and friend, Denis Guiney, have ended up managing Clery's vast department store.

His periodicals included for a while the *Irish Bookman*, under the editorship of J. J. Campbell. It had a short life but a good one. Since the editor was a Belfastman, and a notable one, it was the Dublin periodical that gave the best display to Ulster writers, the only one, perhaps that at that time tried to balance the two cities not against but with each other. It was beginning to create between Belfast and Dublin the sort of intellectual community that could have been valuable. But like many a good idea, including civilisation, it didn't last long enough.

Then there was, or was to have been, the *Irish Music-Lover* with Michael O'Higgins, the great singer, to vet the matter on music: and myself, the dogsbody, standing by to do the journalism. It never got off the ground nor into the heavenly and harmonious air, because, by that time, the end was near, and rising costs were beginning to batter at the market of the upper-class magazine. And not only in Ireland.

His days, and the company he gathered around him, I remember with great affection. Father Gerald who did those marvellous black-and-white drawings of Franciscan life, or the humorous aspects thereof. Richard King, the artist in stained glass. Sam Mulloy and his camera. Máirín Allen and James White and Thomas MacGreevy who were so well worth listening to when they talked about pictures. Larry Egan, the circulation manager. Séamus (J. J.) Campbell, David Kennedy, Seán Feehan, Joe Tomelty, Francis MacManus, Robert Farren, Jimmy Montgomery, Joe O'Connor of Fossa. And a dozen, or more, others.

There were quarrels off and on. He was human. So were they.

But always my memory goes back to that moment and that meeting at that time of life (for me) when a young man has nowhere in particular to go and thinks his experience is unique. There I was, in a state as near to gloom as I have ever allowed myself to be: and muttering about Hilaire Belloc walking in the Valley of the Arun and about how fine it would be to write in that way about well-known, well-loved places. And that stout Franciscan said: 'Take this as an advance. To help you on the road. And go home, and throw a leg over your bike, and cycle across Tyrone and bring me back what you get.'

Which, as I said, I did. And wrote something called 'Long After O'Neill'. Copying a title from Michael J. Murphy who had written in the *Bell*, a fine piece called 'Long After Carleton'.

That was a happy journey. And God and Senan, who sits now at His Right Hand, know when again it may be possible to make such a journey. Even if a hero by the name of Colm Tóibín did surpass Cuchulain by marching all along the Baleful Border, and writing a whole book about his journey.

The handsome, heavily built priest who was chaplain in the 1930s–40s to a certain Dublin orthopaedic hospital and to the nuns and all who ran it, had been a chaplain at the Western Front in the Kaiser War.

His complexion was ruddy. His dark hair was going iron-grey. He was a good sporting shot and almost everywhere he went his dogs went at his heels. His name was not McHugh nor yet O'Byrne but, if put to the pin of his Roman collar, he would have traced his descent, on his mother's side, back to Feach McHugh of the Mountain, Feach McHugh of the Glen, who had defied the armies of Gloriana.

At the Western Front, as war chaplain, the good priest had suffered shell-shock and developed a passion for aeroplanes and, afterwards, flew a small plane until his bishop, no visionary or Amelia Earhart in matters of that sort, grounded him. When he came back to Ireland, and before he took for a while to the air, the principal tourists in Ireland from the other island were the Auxiliaries and the Black-and-Tans, so that he developed, more than somewhat, an anti-British thing.

When I knew him and when he was chaplain to that hospital where I was a patient, the curtain was going up on the Hitler War. Or coming down, black and heavy, on the world.

So he would stand on the sun balcony inhabited by the senior boy patients (myself, who had ceased to be a boy, among them) and he would call out: 'Repeat after me, boys: "England is our only enemy." '

The boys, to the twittering of the nuns and the laughter of the nurses, were only too happy to oblige.

On that day of downpour and thunder when Neville Chamberlain read his quavering declaration, the good priest cried out: 'If Queen Victoria were alive today she would turn in her grave.' And then, to the shaking of his shoulders with merriment, he realised he had said something good.

Because of the lineage he boasted, one of his favourite topics when he lectured to the boys was the ambush in Glenmalure when Feach M'Hugh O'Byrne routed the English and, I suppose, the Queen's Irish, and Earl Grey, and the poet and land-speculator, Edmund Spenser.

'Spenser was there,' the good priest would say. And say it out very loud. And one day a long, lugubrious house-painter from Dublin

City, which was then below there in the hollow and reasonably confined, looked down from the ladder from which he was whiteleading the iron framework of the Vita glass in a corner of the balcony, and said: 'But Father, Herbert Spencer could not have been there.'

The painter had been at the reading: Shaw and Wells and Tressell and all.

And another favourite topic was the quixotic story of the Chevalier Charles Wogan who rescued the Princess Clementina Sobieski from the clutches of the Emperor, which were also the clutches of our only enemy, England. The rescue was effected in Innsbruck and the Princess was brought, by harsh roads and over the Brenner Pass, to sunny Italy to marry James Stuart, the third, and become the mother of Bonny Prince Charlie.

By the whim or humour, surely deliberate if a whim can be deliberate, of the Spanish Power, Wogan was to be rewarded for a life of gallantry, and all the rest of it, by the Governship of La Mancha, of all places in the known world. And to become a correspondent of Dean Swift. Writing like this:

> I know I am a little mad so Mentor [i.e. Swift] must take nothing ill that I say to him. My patience is exhausted and I have done all that I could to tire his. He must blame his own good nature that has given me room to vent my spleen. As I have no friend here of genius or freedom of thought enough to comprehend these notions, they had rolled in my breast if I had not come out with them. I am not setting out on an expedition against the Moors since the modern Christians are too hard for me. . . .

And from Swift's reply and gloriously off at a tangent:

> I have further thanks to give you for your generous present of excellent Spanish wine, whereof I have been so choice that my butler tells me there are still some bottles left. I did very often ask some merchants here who trade with Spain whether this country could not afford something that might be acceptable in Spain, but could not get any satisfaction. . . .

The idea of the Dean and the Chevalier, the last knight of Europe to take weapons from the wall, co-operating in the importing of good Spanish wine, at a reasonable price, into Ireland, is something to play about with. That oddity I recall discussing, in my early days in Dublin, in the Clarence Hotel with both the corpulent Capuchin from Capel Street and the clerical war veteran from Finglas, when Finglas was on the fringe of Dublin City and in the embrace of green fields.

And in the Clarence, and in the grander Gresham as well on occasion, I had the honour to sit, more than somewhat awed, with the great Senan and John Count McCormack, and/or Jack Butler Yeats, or Séamus MacManus, old grizzled storyteller from Frosses in Donegal and widower of the poetess, Ethna Carbery, and Thomas MacGreevy, just returned from Paris with all his memories of James Joyce and many another: *et alibi aliorum plurimorum, sanctorum martyrum et confessorum.*

Who paid the cheque? Senan sometimes insisted. He had patrons who knew he was a good man and great editor and a comfort to young writers and painters.

Some little etchings from those days are still vividly before my eyes.

On O'Connell Bridge I am standing in the evening with the poet, and most learned critic of art and literature: Thomas MacGreevy. He is remembering Paris and mentioning great people. We are looking west and upstream. The sun is setting and bringing dancing, beautiful colours out of the walls of the old brick houses on the left bank of the river. Those old houses are about to collapse with *merulius lacrymans*, the most noxious form of dry rot. In spite of all which, Thomas, the Chevalier as he was by the honour of France, says quietly (he was always a quiet-spoken man): 'Dublin is very beautiful.'

And that from a man just home from gallant Paris.

The old houses have nowadays been restored. But I can still hear the Chevalier praising them in their tottering state, old brick, red sun on the sleepy river: 'Dublin is very beautiful.'

Then the Flying Curate was, as I have hinted, a great man for the dog and the gun o'er the moorland heather, and for the shooting of birds. He had a fine young man who walked with him on such unsacerdotal expeditions. That young man: the son of an Ulster family living in the neighbourhood of that orthopaedic hospital.

Now, in the centre of the semicircle of the hospital's balconies stood the Eucharistic Congress (1932) altar. Not the huge one that had been up for Mass in the Phoenix Park with John McCormack singing

'*Panis Angelicus*' and G. K. Chesterton helping to carry the canopy over the Blessed Sacrament. No, but a smaller, elegant effort that had been used for benediction on O'Connell Bridge in the city centre.

It was a Catholic occasion that drove many of my fellow Ulstermen up the walls: Derry Walls and No Surrender and we'll bate ten thousand Papishers right over Dolly's Brae.

Howandever: this pleasant day the grounded curate is sitting by the bedside of a little boy patient. He is hearing the little fellow's confession. Not much to confess, I'd have said, and he tied down like myself on a Whitman spine-frame. Nothing to do with Walt, the poet.

The young Ulsterman, MacKeever or Sancho Panza, sits at a respectful distance waiting on and for his master. A splendid bird perches on the cross on the peak of the roof of the altar. The confessor leaps up, waving his purple stole and shouting out not *Absolvo Te* but: 'Look, McKeever, there's a great bloody shot.'

The bird hears him and flies away. Could it have been the Holy Ghost?

When I was struggling through college I used regularly to revisit the Flying Curate. All the way to Finglas. My companion, a small dark-headed man with a head full of history. He loved that clerical house. The smell of gun dogs. The two guns holding each other up in a corner behind the hall-stand.

SIXTEEN

Meeting the Queen

Once maybe a score or more of years ago when I watched, on television, the Queen of England, in the north-eastern corner of Ireland, visiting Hillsboro' House and Coleraine College, and attended by her faithful servants, all under arms and parading around that third portion of her far-flung dominions, my mind flew back (there's a fine phrase for you) to visits that one of her predecessors had paid to certain other universities. Predecessor, not, necessarily, ancestor. For you know that royal families, like other and less distinguished families, can go off at a tangent.

I'm thinking now of James Stuart, the Sixth of Scotland and the First of England. You know the fellow I mean: the one who succeeded to Elizabeth Tudor, the First Elizabeth of England, and who was the strange son of that sad and wilful woman, Mary, Queen of Scots. And thinking, too, of the visits he paid to the great universities of Oxford and Cambridge in his capacity as philosopher–king and theologian.

Or as Professor David Harris Wilson ironically put it: Schoolmaster of the Realm.

Or as was said at the time: the Wisest Fool in Christendom.

James was a queer fellow, oh, a very queer fellow indeed. But he had his points. In addition to those that held up his gaskins: see *Twelfth Night*. He had some claim to be theologian, philosopher, and even a bit of a poet. And about his contacts with the universities much could be and has been written. He also had a bit of humour in him as well as a lot of deceit and cruelty. And it was the humour in him that, once in Cambridge, made him so enjoy a jocular disputation on the question: whether dogs could make syllogisms. 'The major proposition, it was argued, formed itself in the dog's mind: the hare has gone either this way or that way, and hence a syllogism was erected.'

The Moderator, fearful for the seriousness of academic debate, tried to stop the whole carry-on. But the King butted in to tell a story about the cleverality of a hunting dog of his acquaintance, and to tell the Moderator to think more of dogs and less of himself. For James was hell for the hunt and followed it even more frenziedly than did even that abominable King, Ferdinand of Naples, whose Queen was friend to Lady Hamilton who was just good friends with Lord Nelson.

When James caught up on a runnable stag that had already been brought down and killed by the dogs, he would cut its throat and open its belly, and trust his hands and sometimes his feet into the stag's entrails, daubing the faces of his courtiers with the blood in token of their sportsmanship and of his high esteem. But, by way of contrast, listen to what King James thought of himself as a peacemaker at a time when he thought, mistakenly, that he and he only would be the God-appointed centre of European peace: 'Come they not hither [meaning: to himself] as to the fountain from whence peace springs? Here sits Solomon and hither comes the tribes for judgement. O happy Moderator, blessed father, not Father of Thy Country alone, but Father of all Thy neighbour countries about Thee....'

In Coleraine, County Derry, Queen Elizabeth the Present could not rise to the like of that, and that reminds me of what I wanted to tell you about:

For the first time Elizabeth II ever came to my native province I met her and this is how that happened. I was then on the staff of a certain Dublin morning newspaper. I won't say which except that it was founded by a man who stood as a symbol of the Irish Republic and that the paper honoured his memory and his politics in every way. You may have guessed.

The editor at the time of the Queen's visit was then, and still is, I hope, a good friend of mine. He was a thrawn fellow Ulsterman. He had done some time in a British prison for a moment of excessive Irish Republicanism. But like the rest of us he had his pleasant and, indeed, jocose moments. So he said to me: 'Would you ever go up to Derry City to cover the Queen and we'll write the heading here and now.'

Which we did. It was: 'No Flags on the Leckey Road'.

That was a shrewd, if easy, prophecy. And the first thing I did when I got to Derry City was to walk up the Leckey Road and into a pub where, in chorus, they were singing the ballad about how the English had hanged Kevin Barry in Mountjoy Jail one Monday morning. And where I was accepted when I showed my newspaper credentials and they realised that, in spite of my accent, I wasn't plain-clothes RUC. So we all sang about Kevin Barry, the Irish martyr, who had been hanged for killing a member of the RIC and I asked a fellow chorister to sketch out for me the royal itinerary for the following day. Which he did.

'She'll land,' he said, 'from a boat at the back of the Guildhall, and go in there and make a few knights, the fellows with the helmets and tin suits. Then she'll go up the hill to a garden party in Brooke Park where they'll all look at her. And then to Eglinton to fly away to Scotland.'

'She won't,' I said, 'have much time in Derry.'

Well, I won't tell you what it was that that Derryman told me the Queen wouldn't have time to do in Derry. But I got his drift as I reckon you'll get mine. Although I afterwards did hear from a Derry lady, who utilised them on the sly, that special regal facilities had been provided in the Guildhall for such activities. That Derry lady and a few of her friends wanted to be able to claim that they had sat where the Queen of England sat.

At any rate, the eve of the visit wore on and we were joined by some of my informant's friends and some of my friends, including Michael Cannon who was then Belfast editor of that paper for which I worked. And many songs were sung-o and the Queen toasted several times. So that on the following morning, the weather being warm, Michael and myself, after our bacon and eggs in the Northern Counties Hotel, were thirsty. An ailment that we disposed of with long cool pints of ale in a lovely little pub close to the Guildhall, and which was then the property (the pub) of a man who was the uncle of a man who was to become a famous playwright. And then out with us to witness the disembarkation of a Queen and Consort. Which was simply accomplished, security being middling easy in those days and, anyway, Michael Cannon knew all the coppers and, being who he was, was known to and respected by them.

Up the hill then in a taxi to Brooke Park where under bright sunshine and in a roped-off enclosure, the Queen and the Prince walked graciously around, and the guests looked at them as if the two of them were about to get rosettes at a show. And the air was musical with the clink of medals on the breasts of bemedalled commanders beloved of the throne. (As John Masefield told me.) Although one cynical journalist, and he was an Englishman, said the hardware was, for the occasion, out of the local Army and Navy Store.

Then at that critical moment in Imperial history, the detritus of the night before and the cool pints of the morning caught up on Michael and myself. So Michael enquired of a convenient constable (remember he knew them all and they knew him) and the constable directed us to the back of a big house that was there in the park, and well within whatever cordon of security there was. Perhaps, under the urgent circumstances, *cordon sanitaire* might be the exact phrase.

We went gratefully and emerged relieved, and saw before us a long line of parked limousines. We stepped out between the second and third limousine in the line to find ourselves standing right face to face with the Queen and the Prince and, back of them, a semicircle of those bemedalled commanders already referred to by Mr Masefield and myself.

What had happened was that while we were relaxing the party had ended and the royal entourage, or equipage or cortège or whatever, was about to move off, and there we two were, surrounded. On a green knoll apart, as another poet puts it, stood a veteran photographer from another Dublin newspaper. A newspaper not then known for Irish Republican sympathies. And that photographer had had a fine record with the RAF in the First World War. But when he saw the humour of our situation he waved his camera with leprechaunish delight and moved towards us. And what he meant was: 'Hold it! Hold it!'

His intention was to get a picture of the two waifs from the Republican newspaper smirking at the Queen and her Consort and, for the hell of it and for more than that, we would have been glad to help him. What a lovely thing now it would be to have to show to grandchildren, and some of them English and Canadian moreover.

But what were we to do? I mean what would you have done? The photographer could not cover the ground fast enough.

So we smiled at the Royal Couple and they did likewise back at us, and slowly we backed out between the second and third limousines. And well it was, as Michael said, and thanks be to God and His Holy Mother, that we were far enough away from the comfort-station at the back of Brooke House to be respectable, and all present and correct, and not to disgrace our rearing and be up for misprision of treason, whatever that may be. Or something worse.

That was the only time I ever met the Queen and, indeed, the only time the Queen ever met me, and she may not, to this day, even know it. For if she had known I might have received an invitation to H. and C., I mean Hillsboro' and Coleraine, on her later visit to those uttermost outposts of the far-flung empire.

Some other time I'll tell you about how Lady Haig walked up Lower Kevlin Road, Omagh, County Tyrone, with a ladder in her stocking. That's all to be part of a book I'm writing, to be called *Royalty and Nobility I have Known*. Or *Now It Can Be Told*.

SEVENTEEN

Margaret Barry in the Brazen Head

O Flora, dear Flora, your pardon I crave,
For it's now and forever I must be your slave.
Your parents they insulted me, both morning, night and noon,
For fear that you'd wed an Inniskilling Dragoon. . . .

The historic dialogue, with more than the suggestion of bagpipe music in the background, between Flora, dearest Flora, and the enamoured Royal Inniskilling Dragoon, used to be one of my own party pieces. That was when the party was well under way. And I used to be mildly proud of my efforts. But I bowed always in humility and held my tongue when I heard it sung by Jack Donnelly, a famous hotelier, when he was manager of the Old Ground in Ennis, County Clare. He was a man who brought song and wide reading and a reverence for ancient places to the hotel business. And his native town was Enniskillen or Inishkilling. Or, properly, Inis Ceathlainn.

And I also bowed in humility and held my tongue when I heard the song sung by the aged Mrs Cooney, mother of Ben Cooney of the Brazen Head Inn in Dublin City. She was the kind of woman Teresa Brayton had been, that Teresa who wrote the exile's song 'The Old Bog Road', and who lies at peace and at home in the old graveyard of Cloncurry to the north of the road from Dublin to Galway and/or Sligo. The Old Bog Road of her most moving song is only a few perches away.

They were both small women, compact, silver haired, with crisp but silvery voices. Teresa, although she had written the words of a song that thousands sang, did not herself sing. But Mrs Cooney did. And, when she sang, it could have been the voice of Teresa singing: crisp, clear, sweet as a blackbird, each word defined and lingered over, and her eyes all but closed, as was the mode once with old people singing in country places. Around her, as she sang, the shadows of caparisoned horse soldiers passed on for ever to Badajoz or Balaclava. And unseen pipers chanted the last farewell.

The summer in the 1950s when Margaret Barry of the Travelling People, with her ballads and her oul' banjo, and Michael Gorman from Sligo with his violin, stayed in the Brazen Head, Mrs Cooney must, by recurring request, have sung at least seven times a week about Flora standing up in her coach for to watch the dragoons parade. She had a verse, too, that I never heard from anyone else: to indicate that after the sad parting there was a happy reunion.

That was a rare summer. As part of it there was the glory of going up one night with Brendan Behan to introduce him to Margaret Barry, holding court like a queen, with Michael Gorman beside her in a triple chair that was part of the Brazen Head's old rare furniture. And of my feeling like some minor God of the Sea, ruler of vast sluice-gates, who had, suddenly and for the first time, sent two lively tides racing together.

With Michael Gorman, the fiddler, I had my own special links. He was one of the great clan of fiddlers of South County Sligo, from the land around Tubbercurry and the parish of Achonry, and Mucklety Mountain and Knocknashee where you can 'wander on to Cloona-cool along the mountainside'. And, above all, the land that held Templehouse Lake. That shy lake, glimmering remotely among deep woods, giving its overflow reluctantly to go towards the sea, by Collooney and Ballysodare, and through the Poet's country, seemed to be the centre of the inspiration of those Sligo musicians, and their finest tune was 'The Templehouse Reel', and the foremost man ever to play it was the renowned Michael Coleman. Who died in the USA. A memory of mine, from the age of nine, is of the music of Coleman, coming from an American green-labelled recording and a gazebo of a long-horned gramophone, filling, in Achonry, a house of the Devaneys who were relatives of mine, and floating on the air around the house, and crossing the fields to the houses of the Rogers family, and the Giblins and the Cryans, and over them all the double peak of Mucklety Mountain, quiet in the purple evening and holding between those peaks memories of the highwayman, Malley Maguire. My cousin, Phil Devaney, had displayed to me in style, Malley Maguire's cave.

It was with the Devaneys that Michael Gorman grew up. It was at the building of a house for a man by the name of Devaney that Michael learned to play the fiddle. His teacher, Jamesy Gannon, wrote out the music for him on ceiling boards that were afterwards built into the house. Music built the towers of Troy.

Michael played, as all the Sligomen did, 'The Templehouse Reel'. But his favourite piece, and the one that (in my expert opinion) he played best was the schottische tune, 'The Chaffpool Post'. It was a dance of spring, advancing, retreating, advancing, coy as a minuet and yet with the promise of love as warm as hayfields.

For me that music had more than mortal meaning because I had learned to ride a bicycle on Chaffpool Hill. A banal enough activity, God knows, but a triumph at the age of nine, and the more so because it was achieved on a high, sloping road that had a view of Mucklety Mountain and Knocknashee and the Ox Mountains.

So with Michael and Margaret and Brendan and Mrs Cooney, and many others, it was priceless to sit in the Brazen Head and let the mind go off on the road round Ireland, as coaches had set off from the Old Inn Yard for many's the long year. There was an account, that I had seen somewhere, dating the Brazen Head back to 1263, almost certainly by a misprint. For the inn would seem really to have emerged from the shadows in the time of the Stuarts. And it had been said that, in her time, Peg Woffington had been there, and Garrick and, more importantly, Robert Emmet and Wolfe Tone and all that delirium of the brave.

Michael's music sent me faster than Ariel and all the way to Sligo. Margaret's rambling tinker talk sent me flying on the circuit of Ireland. And the fact that my elbows were on Robert Emmet's table, then (still) reputed to be part of the furnishings of the Brazen Head, sent me straight away to Kerry where Robert Emmet's pistols were preserved in Daniel O'Connell's house at Derrynane.

Then to be in Kerry was to be in another world. With the famous

Father Griffin of Glenbeigh who had won the Kaiser's Cup at Clounanna with a greyhound called Swanky Lad. Or in Pauline Maguire's of Cahirciveen listening to ghost stories from Port Magee. Or with Bryan MacMahon or John B. Keane in Listowel, remembering Frank Sheehy who died far away in Africa, and how he and Bryan used to maintain that the fuchsia bloomed better on the Dingle Peninsula than anywhere else in Ireland. Or out to Kruger Kavanagh in Dunquin, or to Paddy Bawn Brosnan in Dingle itself. Or standing on lofty Coomakista looking out at the Sceilg Rocks floating in Eternity, a prospect that Bernard Shaw said was the most wonderful seascape he had ever seen. Or listening to fiddle and melodeon in a warm pub in Ballinskelligs and hearing Seamus Murphy, the great sculptor from Cork City, talk of the faces, strong as the stone he worked in, of the men who handled the *naomhógs*, elsewhere called currachs, on those ultimate seas.

Cork, of course, was yet another story. Another story, I mean, from Kerry. There's not a man from Cork nor a man from Kerry who would not agree with me. Nor was there ever a better Corkman to cross with from Kerry to Cork, and back again, than the man I have just mentioned: the sculptor, Seamus Murphy. For all that land is mainly stone carved before time into shapes and symbols. The stones of Cork and Kerry, and the rest of Ireland and All Elsewhere, cry out to and about Seamus Murphy: beginning, say, from the Healy Pass to Cork City, and the bridges over the River Lee, and the stones of Shandon Steeple, particoloured like the people. And on to the old houses high above the narrow, quiet streets of Kinsale where women, wearing meditatively those old black cloaks, seemed to hold to themselves the secrecy of a past of soldiers and battle and high-masted ships. It was a moving thing to stand on a hill high above Kinsale and look out on the convolutions of the sea, and read aloud that passage in 'The Great O'Neill' where Sean O'Faolain at his best, which was better than anybody else, talked of the coming of the Spaniards before the fatal battle that broke O'Neill and O'Donnell: and of the dark-faced Spanish boatmen lifting the long oars in salute.

Back on the road to Cork City is the little river around which Denny Lane wrote that sweet love song:

On Carrigdoun the heath is brown
The clouds are dark o'er Ard-na-Laoi.
And many a stream comes rushing down
To swell the angry Owen a Bhwee.
The moaning blast is sweeping fast
Through many a leafless tree.
And I'm alone for he is gone
My hawk has flown, ochón mo chroidhe. . . .

It was among my mother's favourite songs.

That road also brought one by Crosshaven where Daniel Corkery lived for so long. And by Drake's Pool where that hardy captain came now and again to shelter. A ballad from Margaret in the Brazen Head could, all those years ago, set me off on a long journey. And years later I could still hear her voice and be reminded of places and people.

Six thousand miles away in Oregon where I was for a while, I could close my eyes and see those places quite clearly. This was how and why. A great teacher, under whom I had the honour to sit in secondary school, once said to his wife about me that I would 'go far'. So the good lady told me on the day of his funeral. Out in Oregon I often thought, for the fun of it: 'This is what he meant. If I go any further I'll be on the road home.' And I would look out on the fringe of that illimitable water along which Drake had sailed up as far as the shore of what we call Alaska. And all that, after he had rounded what we call the Cape in a bit of a sailing ship. That same Drake who gave his name to a sheltering pool in the far south-west of my own island. Drake's eyes, also, had watched the Owenabwee swelling to a sheltering salt pool and saw the mighty Pacific rollers crashing on sunburned shores and on green shores of the forest primeval. Drake and myself and Margaret Barry and Stout Cortez and his eagle eye and all his men. . . .

You know what I mean. Or you can guess at it.

EIGHTEEN

Last Waltz in the White Horse

At the foot of the stairs as you descended from the (obviously) upstairs lounge in the White Horse on George's Quay and bang beside that building that had once been the old Tivoli Music Hall, there was a rather wide hallway. And one night in the early 1960s I said to M. J. MacManus, scholar, bibliophile, historian, dear friend, and then literary editor of the *Irish Press*, I said to him that the space of that fine hallway should be put to some use.

'It used to be,' M. J. said. 'It used to be. But that was long before Michael's time.'

By use, I innocently meant a few tables and chairs, or a bench, and a hole in the wall through which, if you opted for a sort of privacy, you could get your drink from the ground-floor public bar. M. J. was talking about something else. For the White Horse, before the gentlemanly Michael O'Connell became proprietor, had had a bit of a wild reputation. About which I tried once to write, calling the pub not the White Horse but the Dark Cow, in a story called 'A Ball of Malt and Madame Butterfly'. That story I built around many stories told me by men older than myself who had known the pub before my time. And known the ladies.

Michael O'Connell changed all that and made the pub dacent. I don't want to use a dull word like respectable. But he kept the pub's merriment and added to it the qualities of his own special friendliness, qualities that his three sons, two in Dublin and one in New York, carefully held on to.

For younger men in the fifties: and that category would have included Gary McElligott, Liam Robinson, Brendan Behan, Alan Bestic, Sean White, Mick Finlan, Breandán Ó hEithir and many another. A most distingished and entertaining throng. And for them all Michael O'Connell was more of a considerate uncle than a businesslike publican. He never showed anybody the door yet the mildest reproof from him was highly and seriously regarded.

For he was Michael O'Connell who came from the good land around Croom in the County Limerick, bringing with him his love of the horses and Listowel Races. And he set up house in the White Horse on the Liffeyside. The name of the house, all the way from the prehistoric symbol on the chalk cliffs of England, must have had a special attraction for him. Back in Limerick in the famous and poetic valley of the River Maigue, his people had known a lot about horses.

It was M. J. MacManus who introduced me to the White Horse and its owner and made me a member of the club, or family. And to make the introduction more memorable to me, Terry Ward was there that night: over from London. He was then London editor of the *Irish Press* and a well-known man around Fleet Street. And he came from the North and from Derry City and when M. J. introduced us he (Terry) said right away: 'You're the young man who wrote a book about Partition and the North. . . .'

I beat him to it: '. . . and knew damn all about one or the other!'

So after that we were friends to the day of his death. All too early.

Like that ancient symbol on the English hills, the White Horse proved, in that particular part of Dublin, to be a stubborn survivor. Consider this list: Tommy Lennon's Abbey Bar, the Silver Swan, Mulligan's, Guiney's, the Scotch House, Phil O'Reilly's, the Red Bank, Mooney's, Jerry O'Dwyer's, the Moore Street Madigans, the Fleet, Bowes', the Pearl, the Palace, the Dolphin. Fifteen in all, if I can count. Eight of the fifteen are gone, and among that eight were my special houses of call when I was a regular newspaperman: as regular as any newspaperman was in those days, before they had good pay and regular hours, and credit lines for summarising the weather forecast.

Others of those fifteen houses of joy and hope experienced transformations, in some cases for the better. The White Horse remained, up to 1980 at any rate, much as it had been except that many of the men I drank with there, thirty to forty years ago, were either dead or cured.

Three things, quite obviously, give a pub its character. The boss and his men. The clients. The quality of the booze. There are incidentals, like standing room, sitting room, ventilation, temperature, sanitation. It is odd that, in our time, while the quality of the incidentals has improved, the general quality of the pubs, in talk and company, has declined.

Every old man says that: remembering the pubs he used to drink in and the company he used to drink with, when, for him, drinking was a new thing. And to be accepted into such company, of older and most learned men, was a never-to-be-forgotten experience. Yet there has never been a great pub in which those three essentials have not been present and as near to perfection as makes no difference. In the White Horse the boss and his men were beyond faulting. Nor was any man ever known to complain about the quality of the booze.

What gave the place its extra-special quality was the mixture and variety among the customers. That set it apart, say, from the Pearl Bar which was close to monolithic: journalists all for Verity's sake, even if the journalists could be noble lords, say Michael Killanin, or sailors home from the sea. The White Horse had its journalists. Inevitably. For it stood next door to the building known in the days of Daniel O'Connell as Conciliation Hall. Later to be known, as I have said, as the Tivoli Theatre or Music Hall, and later, in my days and the days of many others, to house the three *Irish Press* papers, the works and all. But the Horse had, also, the people from the Dublin Docks, genuine dockers and local residents for whom the nearest next town was Liverpool. And there were sailors home from the sea. And a fine selection of the plain people of Dublin.

Therein one night I met a man from Libya, a face much scarred by battle in faraway places, whose special ability was to turn head-over-heels or heels-over-head in mid-air, completely cutting off all contact with Mother Earth but regaining it again with complete nonchalance. Only my dear friend, Butty Sugrue, the Strong Man from Killorglin,

County Kerry who, when he was in Dublin, also frequented the White Horse, had a better party trick than that.

Since the Libyan looked as if he had had a few since he had passed the Pillar of Hercules, Michael O'Connell was doubtful about serving him. Until he displayed his incredible head-over-heels salmon leap. Upon which Michael said: 'Any man who can jump like that deserves a drink.' And poured him one on the house. And included me. Since I was in such distinguished company.

That man from Libya, described as best as I could describe him, you will find somewhere in a novel called *Dogs Enjoy the Morning*. That is, if you can find the novel.

In nearby Conciliation Hall, or the Tivoli Music Hall, the long golden age of editor William Sweetman passed; to be followed by the turbulent years of James Pearse McGuinness. And a new type of contributor to the paper and, consequently, the oddest visitors to the White Horse. One night there were five professors at the bar counter in the upstairs lounge: three from University College, Dublin, one from Trinity College, Dublin, and one from Columbia, Manhattan. And everybody else as usual, and Brendan Behan doing his act up and down the floor.

That particular act was the one about the three patriotic ladies who lay down, all properly clothed, on single iron-steaded beds at the gate of Mountjoy Jail. They were waiting for President W. T. Cosgrave who was due to visit the prison. So when he showed up they called him a traitor to Ireland and demanded that he should have them arrested. President Cosgrave, always a polite gentleman, says, in Brendan's version, that while he may have been a traitor to Ireland etc., etc., he had never been a collector of antiques.

The incident, it seems, may have happened. But it is most unlikely that W. T. Cosgrave ever made any remark of the sort, anywhere or at any time.

In the course of his cavortings on the bar-room floor Brendan had described the three ladies as Oul Wans, a Dublinism by no means unsympathetic or disrespectful. They had been, in all truth, three famous patriotic persons: Maud Gonne MacBride, Mary MacSwiney and a third whose name, for the humour of his act, Brendan did not, for the moment, mention. As he waltzed around he shouted to me to stand up and dance for had I not known one of those Oul Wans. And I had, indeed, once been privileged to stand in the presence of Maud Gonne. Impossible to remember what, in that presence, one had felt or thought or tried to think.

But before I could join him on the dancing floor, one of the professors at the bar counter roared out in splendid voice: 'Brendan Behan, how dare you call my mother an Oul Wan.'

That was R. Dudley Edwards the historian, whose mother, a prominent suffragette, had, indeed, been the third lady. And that act had been arranged between Brendan and the professor to set the whole house laughing. As it most certainly did.

Such moments may have made drinking worth while. Remembering it all, I laugh. Or do I? Nothing remains the same.

I'm getting positively original.

Sometimes, on dull mornings, I used to revisit in imagination old friends, long vanished, in that up-the-stairs lounge bar. But even then I knew, or had heard, that at lunchtime the place was lively and splendid with young business-people from the new office blocks. On pub lunches and coffee. And all that was, and may still be, very good.

But I look back at and see again the floor of that warm, happy room and recall that on that floor I danced my last dance. With Kathleen Behan, the mother of Brendan. An old-time waltz, my limit at any time. With Stephen, her husband, stuffing his pipe in the corner and saying with the utmost equanimity: 'She was faithful to me until she met that fellow.'

Was that the night the singing Clancy Brothers were there? And Kate O'Brien, novelist, and Tommy Woods, diplomat, who as Seán Ó Searbháin and Thomas Hogan and Thersites was also three journalists. Then there were Liam MacGabhainn and Maurice Liston and Arthur Hunter and Michael Mahon, and Routledge and Thompson, and Arthur McGahon and Hugh Madden and Larry Fox. And Mr Martin of the Citizen Army (1916) and his wife, and his daughter, Peggy Morgan. And Mick O'Halloran and Bill Sheedy and Patsy Conroy. And Austin McDonnell of Mayo and 1916 and the Dublin Fire Brigade. And Mark King of Galway. And J. B. Meehan of the British Army and the County Down. And Seamus de Faoite,

storyteller from Kerry. And Colm Brophy, and Vinny Doyle and
Michael Pearse. . . .

*Et alibi aliorum, plurimorum sanctorum, martyrum et confesso-
rum.* . . .

Whatever night it may have been, I did, the next day, as Fusilier
Mulligan put up his bayonet, or so he said, at the special request of
Queen Victoria, I did, I say, hang up my dancing pumps for ever.

NINETEEN

Crossing the Rubicon

It was several years after I had come to know the White Horse that I began working in the building next door. It was not a done thing, round about 1950, to quit a good berth in the *Irish Independent*, then the Great Monolith in Middle Abbey Street, Dublin City.

Adam, we are told, left the Garden under compulsion. But as far as was known, round about 1950, only one man had ever deliberately abandoned that book-lined and easygoing leader-writers' room. He was a man called Seamus O'Farrell, and it was darkly hinted that he had never afterwards been happy in newspapers, and had gone back to the Land and written, from a distance, an agricultural column for the weekly *Standard*. And was even to become a Senator so as to kill the time.

Three men influenced me so that I made the desperate move: myself, George Farquhar, and M. J. MacManus. Myself: because of a misdeed that many people in free Ireland at that time could hardly avoid but that, nevertheless, placed you under suspicion in certain conservative quarters. I had had a novel, *In A Harbour Green*, banned by the Irish Censorship of Publications, God Help Us, for being, 'in general tendency indecent or obscene'. The first of three novels of mine to be so honoured.

And George Farquhar because Lord Longford's Gate Theatre were just then doing one of his plays. And since, as well as writing those deplorable editorials, I also, at that time, did some of the theatre reviews, or notes, or whatever. I had praised *The Recruiting Officer* for, among other things, the strength of its language. Which certain readers of the paper thought was much too strong and they wrote to the editor many strongly worded letters about the questionable morality of one of his theatre critics.

That good man, the editor, who (his successor told me long afterwards) worried about me, did not reprove me. He was too much of a gentleman for that. But I was no longer asked to go to the theatre and a certain uneasiness of mind, in relation to the place I was in, began to affect me.

All of which I mentioned to M. J. MacManus whose solution to my problems was quite simple. Across the river, the Liffey, and not into the trees, but into the land of freedom and with him on the *Irish Press*, de Valera's Irish Republican newspaper.

But one theatrical detail I had almost forgotten. For one last time that good editor did ask me to view and comment on a play. It was Ben Jonson's *Volpone*, and it was Donald Wolfit and in the Gaiety Theatre. At the attempted-rape scene, or whatever, a sincere father, seated close to me, indignantly rose, and escorted his two young daughters out of that house of ill fame. This I later on mentioned to my editor. Who said: 'It's a classic, isn't it? Reduce it to a brief par.'

So, at the request or command of a good man, Ben Kiely reduced Ben Jonson to a brief par.

My friendship with M. J. MacManus, as mentioned earlier, dated from our first meeting, about 1941, when I was a university student and he came to Earlsfort Terrace to chair a debate. And later we were more formally introduced by his dear friend and namesake, the great novelist, Francis MacManus. Our friendship had progressed to the stage where and when I could take my place and feel at my ease in the Pearl Bar with himself and the monumental, in every way, R. M. Smyllie, editor of the *Irish Times*. Although I was never pert enough to call them Joe or Bertie. Those familiar names went back into the shadows of history when, the legend ran, the two of them first met, playing the fiddle against each other in a competition at the *Feis* in Sligo Town.

When people, after M. J.'s sudden death during a golfing holiday on the Donegal coast, would ask me to describe him, I'd say something like this: 'Well, he looked like Charles Bickford, a scholarly Charles Bickford, with reading glasses that had a tendency to work their way down to the tip of his nose. He dressed in a tweed jacket with flannels. He was given to good stories and to rhymes of all sorts: good, bad and indifferent. He had written excellent comical and satirical verse, among many other works. He was kindly, exact in discussion and in opinions, but never much inclined to lose his temper, continually considerate for others, always ready to see the laughter in things.'

Years after his sudden death had removed a light from our world I travelled from one college in Virginia, USA, to another whose president was, as had been M. J., a noted bibliophile, and who said to me: 'Two of your countrymen I knew well. Sir Shane Leslie and M. J. MacManus.' And he talked of the close contact there had been between M. J. and Michael Sadleir.

And then and there, from far away in Virginia, I could see into that corner in the Pearl Bar in Fleet Street, Dublin, and hear the voices of M. J. and R. M. Smyllie, and of the poet, Austin Clarke, and the voices of many others. And remember the regular evening trek of M. J. and myself from the Pearl to Burgh Quay and that office of the *Irish Press*. And hear R. M. saying as we stood up to go: 'Got your leader on Evictions ready, Joe?'

For it was Smyllie's continuing private joke that M. J. was forever writing about the nineteenth-century days of Michael Davitt and the Land League. We'll have the land for the people, as the great song, a favourite with my mother, used to put it:

> They are but a knavish gang that say they own our soil.
> We deny that we were made for them to rob and spoil.
> We refuse to give them what we've won by honest toil.
> We'll have the Land for the People.

That was not quite the case with M. J. MacManus. He was not so comically limited. But on one point Smyllie was correct. In the tiny, brown leather suitcase that M. J. carried and that, in more ways than one, had the stuff of immortality in it, he always, by that time of the evening, had an editorial written and ready: on lined notepaper and in a most exact handwriting. But the topics did vary and only about three times a year had they anything to do with the Land League and Michael Davitt.

Howandever: to M. J. and Smyllie I made my complaint, not too woefully I hope, about the great House of Journalism across the river. And one morning M. J. rang me and asked me would I meet him a little earlier that evening. And not in the Pearl but in the Scotch House. At which I wondered.

And in that ample corner building by the Liffeyside, a famous pub then but now also among the dear departed, and sacred to the memories of Brinsley MacNamara, Flann O'Brien, Terry Ward, Liam MacGabhainn, Maurice Liston and many others, M. J. suggested to me that I might cross the Rubicon and become his assistant. However, he said, to be fair and above board, the great R. M. (Bertie) was also about to offer me a job on the *Irish Times*.

Flattered I was, and no mistake, and I doubt if I have ever been so highly regarded since, nor by two such men. When the matter was signed and sealed we walked to the Pearl and Bertie looked up and said: 'I am told the two of you have been slumming.' Sitting there in his corner he had his eyes and ears everywhere. So we laughed like heroes and drank to the future, about fifty years of which are now in the past.

But before me was the prospect, then to me formidable, of the interview with William Sweetman, editor, and Patrick Kirwan, assistant editor, Scylla and Charybdis, the Pillars of Hercules, of whom I had heard a lot but had never met. But I had once heard about them from Anna Kelly, a great journalist, who said she had learned her English by being secretary to George Moore. As an inevitable consequence she knew all there was to know, and more besides, about gentlemen who wrote novels, and about other matters, and about the types, male and female and in between, or *eadar eathorra*, they mixed with. . . .

Well, I once heard her describe those two remarkable men, Sweetman and Kirwan, as the Unheavenly Twins.

And the next evening I faced up to them: into the shabby old building that had once been a music hall (the Tivoli) and that Kit Scarry, the then works manager, said still was. And before the melodious days of the Tivoli it had been Conciliation Hall where famous political speeches had been made. And whose orators had included Daniel O'Connell, the Liberator. And the men of Young Ireland of 1848.

Up the green, creaking stairway, along the corridor, the newsroom there and, to the right, the engines warming up, and the clatter of the case-room. Whether my eye, at that moment, was or was not serene I do not now recall but I felt actually, and right away, that I was closer to the soul of the machine than I had ever been in the cloistral leader-writers' room north of the Liffey. In which room, Paddy Quinn, the Chief Pol. Corr., said you were permitted to slither or shuffle, but not to walk. And the chief leader-writer, a notable Senior Counsel, had, with wry humour, advised me that on any given night I had a choice between two topics, Godless Russia or The Ratepayers' Burden: 'Write three hundred words on any or either of those topics. And, for God's sake, avoid coming to any conclusion about anything.'

But on Burgh (Burrow) Quay, on the Right Bank of the Liffey, you were closer to everybody from the back-door despatch men to the saintly and scholarly librarian, Aengus O'Daly, aloft, like the saint and scholar that he was, in his library – right under the roof. And from the copy-boy to the Supreme Boss, then that wise statesman, Sean Lemass, and later, as we were all to know, Major Vivian de Valera, son of Eamon who had founded that newspaper in 1932.

Two of the copy-boys I knew became, in later life as we call it, one of them a distinguished painter, of pictures not of houses, and the other a Member of the European Parliament. Messengers of the Word.

But back to that interview: less of a formality than a meeting of men meant to be friends. The only question Sweetman asked (much) was: 'Are you regular? I mean not about your health. But do you come in? Or do we have to send out for you?'

Kirwan talked of a French novelist he was reading and of a brilliant young man on the staff, by the name of Liam Robinson, whom I should meet. And I was later privileged to do so and establish good friendship. Maureen Kennedy, a lovely little lady, who was the editor's secretary, came and went, to ensure, it would have seemed, that the most nervous fellow on earth would feel perfectly at home.

Of all the editors I have met or worked with William Sweetman was, in many ways, the most impressive. I repeat: worked with.

Because he always maintained that you had to have people working with you and not for you. Consideration for his staff in all their works, pomps and miseries marked him out from most men.

A tall man with wild black-grey hair: he strolled, every working evening, casually into the office, always using a side door. Then up a narrow iron stairway and through the case-room, clutching in his hand the paper parcel containing the night's sandwich. There was a legend that because of some odd juxtaposition of stairways he did, one night, use the front door. And the young lady behind the counter in the front office asked him did he wish to see anybody? So he said that he had long hoped to meet Mr Sweetman and he was lucky enough this evening to have an appointment with him. And he went upwards on his way without either embarrassment or offence.

Patrick Kirwan was a grave, quiet man with wide knowledge of the worlds of painting, music and literature. And politics, God help us. He had also studied medicine for a few years. But he was swept into journalism by a whirlwind of a Corkman, a follower and close friend of Eamon de Valera. That was Frank Gallagher, armed rebel in the days of rule from London, novelist, editor, and all the rest of it. Somewhere he had encountered Kirwan and, being a shrewd judge, was quite rightly impressed.

Sweetman expressed curiosity about my former life in the palatial *Independent* building in Middle Abbey Street, across the River Liffey. So I said: 'There are, or were, five of us. We come in at seven and go home about eleven. Except on every fifth evening. When one stays late. To lock up. At about half-eleven.'

He was visibly staggered: 'But that's bad for the morale.'

Then from the end of the corridor which I had just traversed came an astounding roar. Human it seemed.

'That's only Fennessy,' Sweetman said. 'You heard nothing like that in Abbey Street.'

Fennessy I knew already. A decent, resonant man I had encountered in several pubs.

'Faint not nor falter,' Kirwan said. 'Fennessy is famous. He is a link in a long tradition. Beginning, I'd say, in London. *Fraser's Magazine*. MacGinn the Corkman.'

This was an odd world I had walked into. And I was just about able to say: 'The gulf and grave of MacGinn and Burns.'

Which met with Kirwan's sacerdotal approval. And the interview was over.

As I went back to the head of the green creaking stairway, I detoured into the Subs' Room. Fennessy had a point to make, and about everybody. 'This is Dermot Gallagher,' he said to me, 'the man that stuck the *Catholic Weekly Standard* for the death of the Pope.'

Responding to him, and nodding his head in gentle agreement was Dermot Gallagher, one of the wittiest men I was ever to meet anywhere. Beyond a quiet, curious face the epigram was always in the making. With two other memorable men from Sligo, Arthur Hunter and Michael Mahon, Dermot Gallagher went to make up an extraordinary Trinity.

Fourteen or fifteen years on Burgh Quay taught me a lot about myself and others: friends, companions, teachers.

TWENTY

To the Cape and Back

When my good friend, Joseph Tomelty, actor, playwright, novelist and, as Joseph himself would have quickly interpolated, housepainter, first met the publisher, Jonathan Cape, the real man and not just the firm, Joe looked at him with reverence and good humour, and said: 'Mr Cape, I always thought you were your own grand-da.' That odd remark had a definite significance.

Cape, at that time, was just about to publish Tomelty's first novel, *Red is the Portlight*: a novel with its roots in that odd corner of Ireland, the Ards Peninsula where Tomelty came from, and in the little fishing, seagoing, hard-praying hamlets of Portavogie and Portaferry.

That novel fixes for ever in the mnemonic memory that jingle out of a sailor's old randy ballad:

> Ramble away, ramble away.
> Are you the young man they call Ramble Away.

C. V. Wedgwood, the historian (Dame Veronica), had described briefly and exactly what Tomelty saw when he met Jonathan Cape: 'The majestic figure with iron-grey hair rose to greet me. He must already have been in his fifties and I was impressed by his splendid presence: he was absolutely my idea of a distinguished publisher.'

He was older and, if possible, even more distinguished when Tomelty first met him, and when I first met him in the late 1940s.

Tomelty and myself, and many another, had heard the name of

Cape so often that it seemed impossible that the man who owned the name could still be an ordinary living mortal. And in relation to that consideration here is an interesting detail:

> When late in 1927 Alfred Knopf's London office, run by Guy Chapman and Storm Jameson, moved to Bedford Square, they notified booksellers that their trade-department was now, 'five doors south of Jonathan Cape, Ltd'. Jonathan remarked in his house-publication, *Now and Then*: 'It is both surprising and pleasing to realise that we have become a landmark within the space of three short years.'

If an office could become a landmark in three short years it is not surprising that in the late forties, when the chief man in that office was about seventy, he had become as conspicuous in the publishing business as Nelson's Column in the architecture of London.

That latter detail I found, in 1978, in *Jonathan Cape, Publisher: Herbert Jonathan Cape: G. Wren Howard*, by Michael S. Howard, the son of G. Wren Howard, Cape's partner, whose genius for book design, as in the case of Liam Miller here in Dublin, stamped his imagination on a host of books. Michael S. Howard's book was published by the firm of Cape, after Jonathan's death, and was also made available in Penguin.

Now and Then was, as I have said, the Cape house magazine which once upon a time I used to get for free, twice: as a Cape author for the duration of three novels and, also, as the literary editor, God help us, of a Dublin newspaper. *Now and Then* is long defunct, like many another useful publication. And sorry I am this day that I did not carefully hoard my copies. And, as they say, it was in the late 1940s that I first met the man himself, and in the Shelbourne Hotel, and saw exactly what C. V. Wedgwood had described. And I was impressed. More than somewhat.

He was tall, gracious, silver haired, good mannered. But he was as hard as nails: never put twopenny astray, never petted his authors with uproarious advances. And he had a direct way of speaking: not blunt, anything but blunt, just direct and to the point.

On that first meeting he made two statements that disheartened me very much: I was young then. Not statements about myself or my novels (God bless the mark!), the second of which, *In A Harbour Green*, he had just published. No, but statements, very general, about Ireland.

He said: 'Your country, of course, has no economy.' That was not too far from the truth at the time but one did not wish to be reminded of it so lucidly. On the one occasion on which I had had a long talk with the great Taoiseach, Seán Lemass, and when I had had the temerity to reproach him (Reproach? Me? Him?) with his cavalier attitude, or so I thought, to what I called The Arts, he said, with kindly forebearance, that if he couldn't make the country pay its way there would be nothing in it for writers, artists, or anybody else. Thanks to the work and inspiration of that great man a change came about.

The other statement Cape made was even more quenching. He said: 'The Irish situation is no longer of much interest to anyone.' He did not mean to belittle my own dear, sweet country as Owen Roe O'Neill called it: nor to flatten myself. 'It has been remarked,' Michael S. Howard wrote, 'that Jonathan's favourite writers were Irish, American and women – to whom he was always susceptible. While his taste for the first two may have been formed by Edward Garnett, for the third it was all his own.'

Garnett was, as we all know, one of the greatest of publishers' readers: a vanishing breed, now that accountants and public-relations men have taken over the job. What, by the way, is a private-relations man? A father-confessor, a psychiatrist, a blackmailer, a pimp? We'll leave it there?

Once, when Rupert Hart-Davis suggested to Garnett that a book that Garnett favoured might not sell, the reply was: 'My young friend, always remember that there is still in this country a residuum of educated folk.'

When Garnett read for Fisher Unwin he had nursed the talents of Joseph Conrad and W. H. Hudson. For Duckworth he had discovered D. H. Lawrence. Somebody must have seen his Star in the East. Cape? For when Garnett came to Cape: 'He scented out, especially through their short stories, Louis Bromfield, A. E. Coppard, Ernest Hemingway, Liam O'Flaherty, Sean O'Faolain and many others. . . .' He did, it is almost a relief to know, make a few mistakes. But so did the Lord Himself, if He is in it at all.

But it is not my first meeting with Cape, nor his historic career as a publisher, that are on, or in, my mind at the moment. No: but the comic circumstances that surrounded our parting. Not, by any means, a complete parting. For right up to the end, every time he came to Dublin, I was summoned to the presence and hospitably entertained: even though we no longer did business together and I had refused to take his advice about a certain novel of mine, and had gone to another publisher.

The year in which that happened must have been 1952. Wasn't that Holy Year when Brendan Behan and Anthony Cronin set out on sandals, with staves in hands and cockle-shells in hats, on a pilgrimage to Rome: and never got there? See, through laughter and tears, the classic story in Cronin's *Dead as Doornails*.

As for Jonathan Cape and myself: at that time he was holding, but not for the moment wishing to publish, a typescript novel, or something, of mine called *The Cards of the Gambler*.

At the same time a learned friend of mine —

He's still a friend of mine and, in the nature of things, more learned than ever except in the unlikely event of his having forgotten more than he ever learned.

That learned friend, I was about to say, was at that time bound for Peterhouse, Cambridge, to do his doctorate. So for the sake of friendship, and for the joyride, I went with him and we had a merry time on the way.

On the evening of the day on which I left Cambridge to find my quiet and respectable way back to Dublin, I had an appointment with Jonathan Cape: for six o'clock, in his fine apartment at the corner of Bedford Square. He kept that apartment for the meeting of authors and others: close to his office, but just that little apart from the office atmosphere. And in the evening, when the office had formally closed, he could sit in the apartment and talk to guests, or read typescripts until the rush had died down in the Tube and he could go home in comfort.

Howandever: my learned friend and myself are in Cambridge in the morning, walking from Peterhouse to the railway station and just when the boozers are opening. We stop in for a half of bitter. My friend says: 'We'll have one for your road in the pub at the corner.' He is, of course, staying on in Peterhouse. I must rise, as the old song says, and he need not. Then from behind the counter the proprietor of that boozer says: 'Wouldn't if I were you. The pub at the corner, I mean. Full of Irish. Farm workers from a plice called Mayo. Eat you alive.'

We did not tell him. That would not have been plying the gime. My friend had not a noticeable Irish, nor any other, accent, except when he was pretending. And because of the vowel sounds of my Ulster place of origin I have frequently, in southern England, passed as Scottish. Although north of Carlisle the natives would, immediately, notice the fraud.

But we do look into the pub at the corner and find it for us, the mere Irish, rough rug-headed kerns, perfectly normal.

And in that pub I met a tall young man, the wreck of something that had been magnificent, a deserter from the Irish Guards, a shabby man, in ill health, wearing a filthy overcoat that was long even for him. And the neck of a bottle of wine, non-vintage, standing up out of a pocket of the coat: as plain to be seen as the Eddystone Lighthouse. A civil, sad, lost man.

He gave me a message for his brother in Ireland and, later, I am to pass on the message and get little thanks for doing so: and I am never again to see that sad young man. But I am to use him as the basis for a character in a novel called *Honey Seems Bitter*, which Cape, making a special point, is afterwards to mention to me.

All the way back in the train to London I was reckoning that since Cape had asked me to call on him at six in the evening he might be good for a free dinner. That was of the utmost importance. My money, such as it was, was running out and I had to catch the Irish Mail, at Euston Station, at nine o'clock or thereabouts. If (I think to myself) I go down to Fleet Street, to the immortal company of Terry Ward and Con O'Leary, I can raise any God's amount of money. But then I would be happy in Fleet Street, as happy as Dr Samuel Johnson was long before my time, for the next week or more. And I am expected back, in Dublin, about now.

Out of the Cambridge and Peterhouse jollification I had hoarded enough money to get me to Euston Station, to pay on the ship from Holyhead to Dun Laoghaire (I had my return ticket from Euston to Holyhead), to pay my bus fare from Westland Row terminal to Dollymount, North Dublin City which then was my home.

The door of Cape's apartment was opened to me by a charming, middle-aged lady from Galway, of all places, who was a member of the staff. She made me feel almost happy by, obviously, having read a previous novel of mine. As always: the great man was gracious. He produced three varieties of whiskey: Bourbon, Canadian Rye, Power's Gold Label. The Gold Label was a gift from Paddy the Cope Gallagher, great son of Donegal, who was at that moment in London. Cape had published proudly Paddy's remarkable book *My Story*.

So Jonathan and myself sip a soupçon of all three whiskies. The Canadian Rye was, as far as I can remember, a gift from Morley Callaghan. And we nibble Gentlemen's Relish, i.e. bits of toast with stuff on them. The stuff is the relish.

That's the good news.

The bad news is: no mention of dinner. And it's a long, long way to Holyhead, halfways to Tipperary. Whiskey is only a temporary relief. My guts rumble. The worse news is that he thinks I should sit on *The Cards of the Gambler* for a bit. People won't know what it's about. My next novel may be my breakthrough novel. And, after that, he will be able to sell anything with my name on it.

'But,' I plaintively cry, 'I've written the bloody thing. And I need money.'

'Oh, money, money, money,' he said. 'Belloc was always annoying his publishers about money. For his boats. And his wines. Yachts and champagne. Ernest never bothers me about money.'

He was, sure as God, dead serious. And at that realisation, and even in such a presence, my patience broke. Three nationalities of whiskey (or whisky) on an empty stomach. Mercy of God, Neil Gunn and Yukio Mishima were not, in that year, among his authors. Or, to brace me in daring and vigour, I may have remembered something Belloc had, in some golden age or other, written about where to get the blood of kings at only half-a-crown a bottle.

So I rose with dignity, I hope, and said: 'Mr Cape, sir. If I had as much money as you and/or Mr Hemingway I would not be here with my hat in my hand.'

No hat did I possess.

Ernest, God rest the mighty man, was then financially quite comfortable in Havana, Cuba. And might, I felt, at that sad moment, have provided the Bourbon.

All honour, also, to the mighty Jonathan. For we parted smiling and, as I have said, and, in spite of my ill manners, we remained friends. And some months later L. A. G. Strong suggested to John Cullen of Methuen that he might publish *The Cards of the Gambler*. And John Cullen, a perfect gentleman, did.

But I am on the train to Holyhead and it is the Holy Year of 1952.

Three fine Irish ladies on the train tell me how the Pope is doing and ask me to join them for tea. But no, I say, I've just had dinner. Being, at that time, still a gentleman, I feared that if I joined them for tea, politeness might impel me to pay for all of us: and my eyes were on that steak and stout on the boat, and my mind, and my soul, and my rumbling stomach.

At Crewe Junction a noted Irish rugby-football team, with some faithful travelling supporters, joined the train. They were jubilant. They had beaten somebody in Manchester or Brum. One of them carried white busts of Cobden and Bright which they had removed from the foyer of some hotel. At the Customs they declared them as mascots, apostles of free trade, forerunners of the Common Market.

And the Irish Sea was at its worst.

One by one the footballers vanished. Big strong men frequently have weak stomachs on rolling salt water, particularly if their journey has been preceded by overmuch celebratory wine and porter. Over my steak and stout I linger alone, the Last Epicure, and am sick immediately afterwards, my only sickness ever in a boat on the ocean. And, quite unfairly, I blamed it on Jonathan Cape and his Gentleman's Relish.

For the rest of the trip I'm as healthy as a horse and as empty as a whistle. The secretary of that Rugby Club lives in my neighbourhood in Dublin City and he drives me home with my bus fare safely in my pocket.

Money, money, money!

The only profit out of that journey was a short story called 'Mon Ami, Emile', for which I used, also, the misadventures on another journey of a dear friend, the late Frank Henry.

Long afterwards Cape said to me: '*Honey Seems Bitter* was your breakthrough book. You should have been with me then.'

So I told him about the deserter in the Cambridge pub who had found his way into that novel. That interested him: and it interested me to think that he would bother to read a book by one who was no longer with him. A deserter like myself. But who deserted whom? Or did he read that novel just to prove to himself, and to tell me, that he had been right?

Honey Seems Bitter was my fifth novel, I think. Michael S. Howard once wrote: 'For Jonathan a fifth novel held an almost mystical significance. He believed that it established firmly an author's reputation, or made the breakthrough to success if the beginning had been slow.'

Cape also said: 'No publisher ever went bankrupt because of manuscripts rejected.' I'll swear to God and His Holy Mother and the VAT that he did not lose much money by rejecting *The Cards of the Gambler*. An undoubted *succès d'estime*! But he did when he brusquely turned down two novels by William Golding, one of them *Lord of the Flies*. It may be some slight satisfaction to know that Jonathan Cape, like God and Edward Garnett, could make a mistake.

TWENTY-ONE

Three Men and the Whitehorse River

One day in 1971 I walk by the Whitehorse River in the County Laois and remember three men.

Balzac, that decent and overworked man, said about the village on the banks of the Loire where he spent the first three years of his life that 'neither audacity nor magnificence' prevailed there but 'the simple beauties of nature'. André Maurois, in his biography of Balzac, wrote that 'the broad river flowed between sandbanks and leafy islands and the child was happy in that charming countryside'.

Yet it must be admitted that the broad Loire was bordered with magnificent poplars and on the far bank were velvety hills crowned with white châteaux, a very French idea of the simple beauties of nature. By the Whitehorse River in the County Laois there was not, nor is there, anything as grand as the châteaux of the Loire. But the simplicity and beauty are real.

The three men that I remember had enough variety of character to satisfy Balzac himself. Since they were all gregarious men, and since one of them had travelled a great deal in the East, they must have met and known enough people to have stocked another *Comédie Humaine*. That is, I suppose, the pattern of life: Somebody knows Somebody who knows Somebody else so that, in the end of all, Mao and Myself might have been Mates. The three men I'm thinking of certainly knew and respected and liked each other: and I was privileged to know all three of them.

The day is sunny and cold and the daffodils around the house on the low hill behind me are restless in a gentle, nipping wind. One of the three men, Noel Barry, lived in that house, and rejoiced. And how I always envied him: that he had here what he might call his own private trout stream, just there down the daffodil slope, and through one fence and across one field. He was a man of orderly classical mind, and knew all about Cincinnatus and his plough, and about Sabine farms, and knew all the deep-grassed banks that come down to meet the Nore a little below Castletown.

The cattle are curious. Although it seems much too chilly and much too early in the year for any sensible fly to be out of the house, the trout are now and again breaking the water: perhaps just to exercise themselves and keep warm. The roofs of Mountrath and the steeple of the church are over there. Further off, and beyond the graveyard, the Slieve Bloom Mountains are low and brown, not yet blue for summer.

In the coffin before they closed it, he had on his face that slow, tolerant smile, as if he was about to add a footnote to the funny story he had told two weeks before, when we were walking by the sea in Skerries between lectures and discussions at the annual conference of the Peoples' College. He was the sort of man who could smile resignedly at Death. All part of Life. *C'est la Vie.*

At a party in the house of the novelist and playwright, Maura Laverty, when she lived in a Merrion Square mews, I met that man for the first time. That would have been in 1941 or 1942. That was a good party. And it should be easy for me to check on the date because on that very day Maura had got a fat cheque from Longmans on her first novel, *Never No More.* And, like the generous lady she was, she wanted to share her good fortune, and her good humour, with her friends.

The jovial editor of a small magazine did, I remember, do a debagged Highland Fling, shirt-tails flying, on the hearthrug. And because somebody there had just returned from Wisconsin, USA, everybody sang that haunting song, 'Oh Wisconsin, Ah Wisconsin', a sort of state anthem and salute to Wisconsin.

It was summer. It must have been. Because we broke up in a lovely still dawn, the sun coming up. And I found myself walking home with this reserved clerical type of chap who, I discovered as we walked and talked, was coming to work on the newspaper on which I was then suffering. When he asked me what the place was like I said that I suspected it to be an excellent training place for all the mishaps of the future. And I quoted from the less-learned works of the Revd W. F. Marshall (who was also an historian in prose) of Sixmilecross, County Tyrone, from a poem about the mean mountainy farmer, Wee Robert:

> Did ye iver know Wee Robert?
> Well, he's nothin' but a wart,
> A nearbegone oul' divil with a wee black heart,
> A crooked, crabbit crathur that bees neither well nor sick,
> Girnin' in the chimney corner or goan happin' on a stick.
> Sure ye min' the girl for hirin' that went shoutin' thro' the fair:
> 'I wunthered in Wee Robert's, I can summer anywhere.'

That was a quotation he was never to forget.

That morning we walked, although it was a bit out of our way, along Moore Street in the north city, and saw the great gulls rising like raucous ghosts, caught out too late or too early, from the refuse of yesterday's market:

> When grey gulls flit about instead of men,
> And the gaunt houses put on majesty. . . .

Moore Street and the markets are better cleaned nowadays.

The gulls, too, cried over our last walk together on the sea front of Skerries to the north of Dublin City. But not too far to the north.

He had told me, when we first met, that he had formerly taught school as an Irish Christian Brother. His pupils from those days, I was to find out, had some notable names among them. The owners of those names considered that their teacher had been somebody very special.

That day, too, in Mountrath on the Whitehorse River, I shook hands with the leader of a delegation of students who had come down from Dublin from the last school he had taught in. Thirty years after the first wave of students had passed, those young Dublinmen considered that he had been something very special. Like the oddest sort of mirage against the soft green fields of Laois I saw the apartment we had once shared, up in Fairview in north Dublin City: the old, creaking, comfortable furniture, the fireplace halfways up the wall, and the spluttering wartime turf (peat) sending what heat it produced up the wide chimney and in the general direction of the moon, but never, no never, into the living-room.

Our arrangement was that he did the cooking and I did the cleaning. He was a good plain cook. But the cleaning done was minimal for the cleaner had a theory that if dust was left long enough in a quiet place, like under the bed, it solidified, and all you had to do was pull it out, roll it up like a carpet and carry it away. Once or twice that theory was almost proved true.

It was wartime and the oddest things were to be found in tins. As a submarine captain might have said when the depth-charges came wobbling down. Once in our mess of pottage we included something (out of a tin) that turned our teeth so black, quite utterly black, that it took two weeks of ferocious scrubbing to whiten them again.

On such absurdities can a lifelong friendship be founded. He was a man of many and varied and enduring friendships.

There is a cloud now up on the Slieve Bloom Mountains, just above where the infant River Barrow, or part of it, leaps in pools over the rocks at the Catholes. Can such low modest hills really produce two great rivers? The Nore and the Barrow. Do the rivers know when they tumble down over the mountain stones and go their own ways that before they meet the sea, 'salt and redeeming and cold', the unalterable laws of clay and rock and contour will bring them together again?

Here on the bank of the Whitehorse River, which becomes a small part of the River Nore, I walk with my memories of three men.

The second man of the three was a lawyer, Eamonn Crowley. Behind his desk he was a gruff, exact man, intent on getting at the truth but only so that he could help the people who came to him for help. He thought more of people than he ever did of fees. After his death people that I never even knew he knew told me how good he had been to them.

And away from that lawyer's desk he was a humorous, talkative man, well read in a way that had nothing to do with books of law, always generous, given to the odd ballad and the recital of verse. He was the only lawyer I ever knew, or am ever likely to know, who could recite, word perfect and in its entirety, George Meredith's 'Love in a Valley'. His favourite quotation, though, as all who knew him will well remember, was the third verse from Donagh MacDonagh's 'Song of the Marshalsea Debtors'. And as long as Donagh, who was a non-practising lawyer, and my lawyer friend are remembered, that verse will be quoted:

> A dark eye or a grey eye, an eye that's soft and tender,
> A form that's tall and slender, a breast that stands at bay,
> An ankle trim and shapely, a hand that's slim and playful,
> A mouth that's shaped for kissing and breath that's a bouquet.
> These are the charms that ruined me, yet I pursued them foolishly,
> Certain that each new schooling would give me my degree.
> But all a lifetime brought me, the first girl could have taught me.
> For all I ever learned of them was what they thought of me.

That man and myself had a friend once (we had many friends), a man in passing, a Spanish poet by the name of Alfonso Costafreda. And as Irishmen, doing our best to be proud of our country, we showed that man from Barcelona a lot of Ireland. We could always laugh to remember the day, in a pub in Mullinavat, when the poet burst the back of his shirt in his eagerness to display to two old ladies in shawls, who were sipping porter by the hearth fire, what flamenco dancing was all about. He was a fine poet and a splendid flamenco dancer.

Long afterwards I had in Atlanta, Georgia, USA, a student from South America, who had met and read Costafreda, and had heard him tell the story of his life and times in Ireland and of that great good-hearted lawyer.

Somebody always knows somebody who knows somebody else.

The third of those three men was a journalist, Kevin Aspell, a much quieter man than the other two, sailing his small boat, you might say, and leaving the surface of the stream as unmarked as that smooth pool there at that deep bend of the Whitehorse River.

He had been sent to an English public school and had the accent that went with that. He had worked a lot in Singapore and Eastern places where he said, with humour, his accent at that time was a sort of protective colouring.

'They would ask me,' he would say, 'how was my war. And I would say that I had had an unusual sort of war. That, generally, was enough to halt queries for the time being. They may have thought that I was hinting at some sinister, dangerous, official secrets. How could I ever have told them that I had been a corporal in the Irish Army and that I did my toughest service playing poker and drinking bottles of stout in a gun shelter on Howth Head.'

But the biggest adventure in his life, he said, had been when, after a heavy lunch in the famous Red Bank, he fell asleep in the stalls of the Theatre Royal, Dublin, half woke up suddenly, and stumbled by error into the wrong comfort-station. And had to spend hours there hiding in a cubicle until the foyer (so to speak) was empty of ladies and he could make a dash for it. And to walk out when the theatre lights were on, and he in full view of three thousand people.

He said: 'Nobody saw me. Nobody expected to see a gent emerging from the powder room. G. K. Chesterton had it right. People don't see what they don't expect to see.'

Three men who loved laughter and who often laughed together and who went, within a few days of each other, into what Wordsworth called the incommunicable sleep. Here by the banks of a stream that one of them loved they are exalted for ever in my memory. Their friends will know them.

'Darker grows the valley,' the lawyer recites to me, 'more and more forgetting. . . .'

The Slieve Blooms have gone back into the mist which is really the evening. The daffodils on the hill around the house are not stirring any more.

TWENTY-TWO

'You Must Meet Seamus Murphy'

At the age of fourteen, as Seamus Murphy told us in his book *Stone Mad*, a book that is one of his many monuments, he was sat down before a block of soft stone and asked to carve a tulip. He was given a lovely red tulip as a model and was on his way to becoming a stone carver: 'The only legitimate stone-carver turned out in Cork in twenty-five years.'

That picture stays in the mind: the boy, the red tulip, the block of soft stone to serve as a bench and be known as a banker. There was a lot of Seamus in that picture: the matter, the form, the beginning of a long intimacy with stone – and, also, the humour that went with that picture of his early days. He said that he was small for his age and that some of the seasoned stone-carvers in the stone-yard thought that he had simply come in there looking for a ball bouncing and lost in schoolboy play on the street outside.

It was Francis MacManus, the novelist, and Peter O'Curry, a newspaper editor, who first said to me: 'You must meet Seamus Murphy.' And with a raised tone of surprise in their voices as if they were saying: 'You mean to tell us that you have not met Seamus Murphy? Nor have you seen the Rock of Cashel, nor heard the chimes from Shandon Steeple which is particoloured like the people.'

Then Máirín Allen, the art critic who, about that time, was writing a series of studies of Irish artists for the *Father Mathew Record*, talked about Murphy incessantly and with affection and enthusiasm. Father Senan, who was her editor, and Thomas MacGreevy and Michael O'Higgins and Michael Bowles and Richard King made regular laudatory references to him. A man much respected and loved, I reckoned, by all sorts of people. That, you might say and as I found out as the years passed, was a modest sort of conclusion to come to.

Our first meeting came about in an odd way. That was in the spring of 1947 and the day was a Saturday, bright and cold. A group of us in Dublin, including Patrick Kavanagh, Anthony Cronin, Kevin B. Nowlan, had been walking the town: a thing one could easily do then without being knocked down and rolled over by motor cars or trampled on by flaming youths. Somebody met me, in the course of our learned parade, and told me that Seamus Murphy was up from Cork and was, to my great gratification, looking for me. Something to do with the book I had written about William Carleton.

The party of us, on that cold and invigorating day, finally came to rest in the Pearl Bar in Fleet Street. If anything could be called rest that had to do with the company I was in. The topic of conversation was historical and K. B. N. was holding forth, against some heckling, as he was perfectly entitled to do. In a lull in the elegant and learned conversation I took off for the Gentleman's and found myself side by side with a man who had just stepped in and up the stairs from the street. He reached me his free hand and I did likewise, and I had at last met Seamus Murphy: the beginning of a friendship that Death Himself does not seem to have interrupted. There are certain people you can go on talking to for ever.

Thereafter every meeting with him was a joy to be looked forward to and to be remembered and talked about afterwards. Some meetings, as is the way in such things, were more memorable than others. There was a library conference in Galway City that involved, naturally enough, many notable librarians, a fine race of people: among them, on that occasion, Robert Herbert of Limerick City, Sam Maguire of Galway County, Dan Doyle of Limerick County, Paddy Madden of Cork, Máirín O'Byrne of Dublin City and County and, above all, Diarmuid Foley, then of Cork City and a most zealous promoter of the genius of Seamus Murphy.

For extra special value we had the company of that great novelist and great lady, Kate O'Brien, and, also, an involvement in the wedding party of a beautiful young lady from Gort who is, by now, a settled and happy matron. Jimmy Walsh of the *Tribune* was doing the pictures of the occasion.

Then there was a memorable night by the Cross of Spiddal and a memorable journey to Maam Cross and into the Great Beyond of Connemara: with Seamus stopping here and there to examine great roadside rocks and to discourse on the nature of the stones of Ireland or, rather, the stone of Ireland. For all stones, he might point out, though different ages and characters, are of one family, the strongest and most respectable on earth. Beyond and before them and underneath them there is only the creating and destroying fire.

It would be a pitiful euphemism to say that Seamus Murphy knew Ireland only from the ground up. And that day at Maam Cross, in the heart and soul of the West, I had a vision of the great sculptor turning those roadside rocks, one by one, into splendid shapes and figures: as certain Americans, intoxicated by the size of their own country, had done at Stone Mountain in Georgia and at Mount Rushmore in the Far West.

In his conversation Seamus refined the sharp wit of Cork City to a sort of half-honeyed, sparkling wine. Some of the things he said to me I have repeated seventy times over and always with due acknowledgement. For three reasons. One: I'm an honest man, at any rate about copyright. Two: what Seamus said would not sound the same in an Ulster accent. Three: it was, and is, always good to mention his name and tell people about him.

For instance: under the towers of Notre Dame de Paris I once told an elderly American lady how Seamus said his father always bought two copies of 'D'Echo' (i.e. the Cork *Evening Echo*), and read both carefully in case he would miss anything in either. The good lady was so taken by the idea that she there and then bought two copies of the continental *Herald Tribune* from a newsboy: a Danish student who happened to be a friend of mine.

And talking of echoes: there are so many places in and around Cork, and Dublin, and around Ireland, that still hold for me the echoes of his quiet, lilting voice, reminding me of the warmth of a friendship that one encounters but seldom. There is the valley of the River Lee as you go to the West, and Seamus talking about his father and the men who went out with the beagles in the early morning. (If you want to know how he talked read *Stone Mad*, and out loud, and try to imagine that the Lord Above has blessed you with a Cork accent.) Then there was an evening in the town of Macroom, and big-booted men and women coming in from the hunt, and every one of them glad to be recognised by the sculptor.

Or on to Ballyvourney where his statue of Gobnait of the Bees presides over the holy peace of the place where Donal Cam Ó Suilleabháin passed in pilgrimage in days not of peace but of deep distress. You can think a lot about Seamus Murphy there, as you can in Stephen's Green in Dublin when you look at the head of the Countess Markievicz, modelled on the head of another Sligo lady, Máire Noone. Or in Gougane Barra itself; for no man felt more deeply than Seamus did the wrong that was done to the Tailor, that grand old man of the holy valley, and to Eric Cross who wrote the book about him. Delicately the sculptor preserved in his work the alert genius in the face of that talkative old man.

But the best place of all to meet Murphy was in his own home, high on the hill overlooking the flat of Cork City: and there was no one who knew him well who does not remember long delightful evenings of talk and hospitality there. Perhaps because they were so delightful Seamus and his wife, Maighréadh, must have suffered a fair amount, not only from the continual intrusion of their friends but from the tendency of their friends to say to visiting strangers: 'And you can't pass through Cork without meeting the Murphys.' The perfectly sound assumption was that no visit to Ireland could be complete without meeting them. Yet the wastage of the time of two busy people must have been considerable. They never complained.

Then to go down the hill and walk the flat of the city with Seamus was really something. To his workshop in Blackpool where the shapes of Ireland were emerging, stroke by stroke, from the stone. And to the church he designed for that Renaissance man (as the poet, Patrick Kavanagh, once described him), William Dwyer, the industrialist: a church that, unlike many others in Ireland, grows up like nature from the ground it stands on.

Then along William O'Brien Street, dear to the heart of Joe Lynch, and to listen to all the stories of old Cork that that unusual thoroughfare provokes. And on to the Old Butter Market and

Coppinger Row and then up Shandon Steeple. Once on the steeple we encountered a young minister of the Church of Ireland who was so new to the cloth and to Cork that he did not know who Seamus was. Very politely that young man told us all about Shandon Steeple and the stone it was made from. Most courteously Seamus listened as if he were hearing it all for the first time. He would not for the world have hurt the young fellow.

The last time I came into the Cobh of Cork was by water, and from across the broad Atlantic. Seamus and Maighréadh were there to meet me. To be welcomed home to Ireland by the Murphys made that day a day to be remembered for ever. It was at the end of the great summer of 1968, and I travelled the rest of the way to Dublin in a mood of exultation as beautiful as the countryside around me. For various reasons it will never be possible to have that experience again, yet with the passing of the years, the memory grows more vivid.

TWENTY-THREE

St Kilian and the Rising of the Moon

J ust once I was in Wurzburg and my memories of it are splendid: the noble city itself, the light, white Franconian wine, the tall Franconian women (their appearance I merely mean), the sculptures on that fabulous bridge, the luxury hotel I stayed in (I wasn't paying), and the then recently restored city museum and its quite remarkable curator.

To begin with: What was I doing there, and why was my bill being paid in a luxury hotel in one of the most splendid of German cities?

It was the year Dr T. J. Kiernan, a quiet, scholarly man and, from the first day I met him, a good friend to myself, went to Bonn as Irish ambassador. My first meeting with him was in the 1940s, just after the war (that war) was over, and he was on his way between Rome or the Vatican, I can't remember which, and Canberra. And I went to the temporary apartment he and his family had in Dublin to gather material for an article about him for a certain magazine.

As far as I remember, that apartment was on the side of St Stephen's Green that in the late 1970s was put in peril by what are known as Developers. It looked then as if it might remain for ever in a shattered and undeveloped condition, with only the College of Surgeons, which survived even the guns of 1916, and a beautiful small church, to keep a good look on that portion of the face of the city. Today, though, that side of the Green looks splendid.

Howandever: the day I went to that side of the Green to meet Dr

Kiernan for the first time had, up to that moment, been for me a long, cold, wearying, harrowing day. A hungry day also, because, through no fault of my own, I had missed lunch, a thing I had long ago taken a pledge against doing. A pledge I have kept to the best of my ability.

In the kind and easy way she had, T. J. Kiernan's wife looked at me and said: 'You could do with a hot cup of tea.' Three minutes later she said: 'You could do with something in the tea.' Thirty minutes later: 'You'll stay for dinner.' Which, feeling much better, I gladly did and laid the foundations of friendship with two wonderful people.

The lady was famous under her maiden name, Delia Murphy, the singer, who with Colm O'Lochlainn, publisher and professor, and Donagh MacDonagh, the poet, did so much, at that time, for the revival of balladry and folk music. Something that seems easily forgotten at a time when five hundred or more groups, most of them deplorable, are roaring their beards off and ruining good guitars.

But back to Bonn which was, when I first visited it, still in its infancy as a centre of government and diplomacy. The hoary joke that must have been made about many quiet places – and I even heard it made about Durrow in the County Laois – was still going the rounds in and about Bonn. This was it:

An American journalist, a political correspondent, arrives in Bonn and when he has dined well asks: 'Where's the nightlife?' And is told: 'She's gone to Cologne for a night off.' Except that, in the case of Durrow, the answer was, or was vilely suggested to have been: 'She's gone to Kilkenny to the pictures.'

At any rate, the new ambassador was not a man who was madly in love with diplomatic capital cities, even if Bonn and Rome he reckoned among the best that he had known. Washington DC, he said, was the worst, and reeking with indescribable snobberies. Canberra had been good, because it had been so bad and he had disliked it so much that he stayed out of it as often as he could, and thus saw a lot of Australia and Australians, which and whom he loved.

Never having been a diplomat myself I wouldn't know anything about these matters and only repeat what, in private, he told me. So his first action in Bonn was to plan a tour of the major German cities. And the West German government was pleasant enough to ask three Irish journalists to go along with him.

It was a splendid journey. Great cities, even if here and there they were still heroically struggling to emerge from the rubble: glorious landscapes, rolling rivers, good company and good wine. And I have such memories of Bonn and Dusseldorf, Wiesbaden, Hamburg, Bayreuth where we had lunch with Wagner's nephew and a beautiful (female) opera singer, and saw and heard a rehearsal of *Tannhäuser*. And I had the odd experience of sitting in the seat in which Adolf Hitler, may he rest in peace, sat when he came there for solemn music.

And memories of West Berlin and even East Berlin where the ambassador, looking around in a bookstore for something to give me by which to remember the occasion, picked up a copy of the Frank Norris novel, *The Octopus*, very apt, on which he wrote his name and the day and the date. I have it still or, rather, my son has it, which is better and makes for longer memory.

And Wurzburg of St Kilian where my tall humorous journalistic colleague and myself sat down, on our arrival, in my luxury hotel bedroom and sipped a little restorative diplomatic whiskey thoughtfully provided for us by Dr Kiernan. He seldom or never touched it himself but he knew that wandering men who have no parish of their own, at the end of a day of travel and German food *go flúirseach*, and German wine which was fine but, in the end, like all wine, a soporific, could do with a little something to make the spirit sparkle.

As the great Jules Michelet said about coffee.

To us as we sipped, and solicitous about our welfare, came the manager of the hotel. And led us, having sipped a little himself and pronounced it *wunderbahr*, on a solemn tour and inspection of my bedroom suite. My companion had a similar set-up next door. There were three forms of bath in my bathroom and, for all I know, if you wanted to have a bath while standing on your head that, also, might have been possible.

As a man from the Far West (of Ireland) once said when he saw the facilities in the modern urban home of a friend of mine, a TV personality: '*Is iontach na jacks a bhíos ag na daoine uaisle.*' (It's wonderful lavatories the gentry have here.)

The bed was asphodel. The fittings shone, but with discretion. The manager hoped that everything was to our satisfaction and he wished for us to be as comfortable as we would be at home. At which, I regret to say, we laughed out loud. Not that we were badly looked after at home. But the Wurzburg style, or the style of that hotel, I had never before, nor have ever since, seen the like of, by land or sea or in the air.

And I may add that, being wise newspapermen, and old dogs for the hard road, we had resolved at an early stage in our careers that, while working and travelling we should, at least, never be less comfortable than we were at home. Since munificent Irish newspaper managements were, mostly, footing our travel bills we were allowed latitude in luxury and it was easy for us to stick to that resolve. (Laughter.)

Then there was the Wurzburg museum and the curator thereof. As for the white Franconian wines and the tall Franconian women, I pass their bouquets and their buckles by.

As far as I recall what had been the museum had copped a bomb. They were delivered by air in those days, and in the face of gunfire, and not by sneaky guys or in stolen motor cars, nor by innocent people bullied or blackmailed into doing the delivery, the most dangerous part of the dirty work.

Anyhow: the learned curator had reorganised the show in a most extraordinary medieval building that had once housed the horses and horsemen and soldiery of the prince–bishop of the place. Something like that. A most impressive building and a most impressive man to look after it. He was short of one arm from the Hitler War. On his cheek he had a sabre scar, the genuine duelling mark which once, in Germany, you were literally bloody nothing if you were without. He was such a fine handsome fellow that I'd say anything that might happen to him could only add to his air of distinction.

And he knew an awful lot. And I had the misfortune to be walking ahead and alone with him when he cut loose on St Kilian in that museum.

'He made us Christians,' he said. And added cheerily: 'We murdered him, you know.'

There and then I was up against a difficulty that has often confronted other Irish people in other European places: that we, in fact, know so little about those Irish saints who made their hallowed missionary marks eastwards. St Fiacre, say, or St Gall, or even

Columbanus himself about whom, we must not forget, Francis MacManus wrote a good book. Occasionally a preacher may get eloquent about them. Wasn't there a story about a decent man in Cork who talked from the pulpit for the most part of an hour about what Irish monks had done for Europe in the Dark Ages, and then wound up with this grand salamander: 'That's not religion. That's fact.'

A good lady who heard him told me that she sneaked a look around to see had anybody noticed. But not a face-muscle twitched. Everyone was in his, or her, own separate trance, separate world of Sunday-morning mesmerism.

But there I was in faraway Wurzburg and a learned German talking to me about St Kilian and his successful mission, and how he was martyred with two companions. And I couldn't keep up my end of the conversation. All I knew about St Kilian was that, like T. P. MacKenna, a gentleman and a celebrated actor, he came from Mullagh in the County Cavan. Then I had a vision and, like better men than myself when in such a state, I saw a book: a shabby little faded red book, six inches by four, one hundred and forty pages, stained by age and use, given to me as if it were gold-dust, as indeed it is, by my dear friend, William Walsh, elder brother of Michael Walsh, the poet of Fore in County Westmeath: and not that far from the circular (round) lake of Mullagh on which Kilian must have looked, as St Colmcille did on the spreading Foyle, before he crossed the ocean.

On the cover of the book a harp stamped in gold, also faded, and round the harp a circlet of leaves, all faded gold. The title of the book, *A Wreath of Shamrocks*. The author's name is Leo who was John Keegan Casey, that Midland poet who, as I cannot too often repeat, is not to be confused with John Keegan, the Laois poet, or more importantly still, the Laois storyteller.

The little book, which is here beside me, opens almost automatically at 'The Rising of the Moon', mostly, but sometimes at 'Carroll Bawn', sometimes at 'The Reaper of Glanree'. By Midland hearths many songs were sung out of it before it came into my possession. But in Wurzburg in vision I saw it opened at another page and my memory read:

Nursed beneath an Irish mountain by an Irish mother's hand.
Where the mild Borora whispers to the meadows of the land,
Taught the music of the harper and the anthems of the blest,
Kilian grew, as grows the ash-tree by the rivers of the West.

For John Keegan Casey did write a long narrative poem, one hundred and twenty-eight lines, about Kilian. And that day in Franconian land John Keegan Casey nobly came to his countryman's rescue. When he was, for patriotism, on the run in Dublin City it was said that Keegan Casey (Leo) went about dressed up as a Quaker. In Wurzburg I didn't see how he was dressed, but grateful I was for his aid and for the gift William Walsh had given me:

How St Kilian's name was honoured in the mystic German land,
How the pilgrim read his history in cathedrals tall and grand,
Sung the silver bells of Wurzburg in a peal of melody,
Through the blue mist of the twilight, as the tale was told to me.

TWENTY-FOUR

Brendan Behan's Coral Island

T he news I read one day that three thousand women had been seized on the Border by Customs Officers as they were being ferried into the Irish Republic in the neighbourhood of the town of Dundalk (known for some time now as 'El Paso') recalled to me at the time my first reading of *Borstal Boy* in the year of publication, 1958. If you doubt my word about the Sabine incident then read it as I read it in the Dublin *Evening Herald* for 18 October 1981:

> Hundreds of copies of an international best-selling book dealing with the sex lives of over 3,000 women seized by Customs Officers as they were being ferried into the Republic near the Border at Dundalk.

Sic! As gentlemen used to say in the days of classical scholarship.

On the evening of the day on which the quite ludicrous Censorship of Publications banned *Borstal Boy* for being 'in general tendency indecent or obscene', Brendan came to me, where I then worked in the *Irish Press*: and he was in a considerable state of just wrath. Since I had already appeared on the banned list (it was then almost a disgrace not to), he could be assured of a brotherly welcome: besides which we were friends if not quite, as the Borstal boys would have it, chinas. The gravamen of his complaint was that in his own town his book should be so slighted by a parcel of bogmen hiding in a room in (as far as I recall) Fitzwilliam Square. As a matter of strict accuracy, I doubt if they were all bogmen. Anyway, on this matter of rural types his tongue spoke louder than his heart: and once he made to me, with remarkable joviality, this statement. The words I recall exactly, I can still hear them:

'I want to tell you something. I have a pathological horror of country people. And no offence to yourself or James Pearse McGuinness [then editor of the *Irish Press* and, like Brendan himself, an old IRA man, though by no means – nor was Brendan – of the breed now in fashion], but the North of Ireland country people are the worst. There are two types of North of Ireland people: the Protestants and the Catholics. The Protestants are all right. Up where they are, they've grabbed everything. So they stay at home and don't annoy you. But the North of Ireland Catholics, they have to go somewhere, and a lot of them come to Dublin and they'd lift the sausage off your plate.'

As I say: it was all stated with the greatest joviality: and that pathological horror, a ghost out of childhood, existed simply, even if not too seriously, because on his streets of the Northside, the representatives of authority, the teacher and the policeman (Garda), were almost always countrymen.

Anyway: on the evening of the banning from Dublin of Brendan Behan his *Borstal Boy* (Ungrateful Florence, Dante sleeps afar. . . .), we went from the *Irish Press* to Michael O'Connell's The White Horse, which was then the sub-office: and from thence to Jerry O'Dwyer's in Moore Street to meet Philip Rooney, one of the last of the gentlemen and the novelist who had written *North Road, Captain Boycott* and *The Golden Coast*. Against those banning bogmen Brendan's complaints were loud and persistent: and a stranger at the bar counter beside us, encouraged perhaps by my own accent, said to me in a voice straight out of Watson's quarry, which is somewhere between Omagh and Mullaghmeena: 'What's it all about? What's ailing your friend there?'

Philip Rooney explained.

Then my fellow provincial asked Brendan what size was the book and was told that it was a middling big book. 'But I mean how big is it, exactly.' And he made gestures that indicated length, breadth, thickness.

We were thoughtful: this, at that time, seemed the oddest approach ever to the evaluation of literature, although it is now quite standard practice in the blockbuster business.

So Brendan gave him to the best of his memory and ability the required dimensions, and the man said: 'Say the word and I'll run you over two thousand of them.'

He was, as it was revealed, a butter smuggler and one of his many and main concerns was cubic content: how many boxes of butter, each containing twenty-eight packaged pounds, would fit on to the back of one agile truck. They say that in Crossmaglen that used to be a problem in the primary-school arithmetic: and the interesting thing was that that man who, if required and if still alive could move an EC butter mountain, was deadly serious about the books. Brendan for a brief moment was stunned to silence but not into the folly of laughter. We had another round and we explained the other aspects of the problem. Later on Brendan sang: 'The Bonfire on the Border', which was then a funny song.

That was in the week of my first reading of *Borstal Boy*, apart from bits of it that I had read, and heard, in advance. For Brendan never felt bound by the cautionary advice given by some cold somebody-or-other: 'Never tell a story, or you may never write it.' A wiser advice could well be: 'Do not tell a story to a man who may write it for you.'

My second reading of the book was in the summer of the year 1964, whose spring saw Brendan's death: and I was reading the book with a class of young women in Hollins College, Virginia, but also reading it to myself, and sadly, in the silence of the southern night: silent except for the multitudinous grasshoppers.

On my list of recommended reading for that class I placed *Borstal Boy* after James Stephens's *The Crock of Gold*, since I thought, before I left Ireland, that the shock of contrast might keep the students aware. They were a most intelligent group and needed no awakening shocks and took the Borstal Boy straight away to their hearts and minds: and one of them told me that community readings from the book were going on in the elegant houses in which the young women lived.

They were, not surprisingly, impressed by words not customarily in use in respectable American houses: but much more they were impressed by the author's vast and obvious humanity, by his humorous acceptance, his abounding life and love of life. His people,

from the roughest screw in Walton to the gentlest boy in the open
prison camp by the North Sea (and with the possible exception of the
RC chaplain who, quite without authority, cut him off from the
sacraments), are almost all looked upon with sympathy, or, at any rate,
with a sort of pity ('for very oft we pity enemies'), or with a defensive
enmity that becomes perverted brotherhood. You feel that if the worst
of them had met him elsewhere, and under less claustrophobic
circumstances, the unpleasant things might not have happened.

One of those women in Hollins, Virginia, who had thoughtfully
read the book, queried me about Brendan's father and mother: and
glad I was to be able to enlighten her about those two wonderful
people: and to return in the book to one of the several perfect little
etchings of Stephen Behan in his humour:

> I dug a field once with my father, the time of a strike, when the
> Dublin Corporation gave the men plots of one-eighth of an acre out
> on Dean Swift's in Glasnevin. My old man dug a good bit of the
> field, with great function, and talked about the land and how our
> ancestors came from it and how healthy it was, and saying that we
> could easily find relics of Swift or Vanessa and Mrs Delaney and
> Stella as we dug, but, after a while, he got bored, and the next day
> he got a countryman to dig the plot in exchange for my father doing
> two turns on picket duty.

Conditions in that Borstal institution were better than could have
been expected, for the governor seems to have been a most unusual
man: and he afterwards remembered and spoke well of his most
unusual pupil, or protégé, or whatever. Yet it still took a warm nature
to turn a prison journal into something not unlike R. M. Ballantyne's
The Coral Island. When Brendan and Jock and Charlie and Chewlips
defy the regulations and the mines of the Hitler War and go skinny
dipping in the North Sea, the reader is almost deluded into thinking
that he, or she, is sharing the best holiday that Brendan, or anyone
else, ever had.

He was never one to grouse or begrudge: nothing ever in him of the
sad types who, if they had a thousand nicker and Rita Hayworth in the
Dorchester Hotel, would still find something to complain about. On
two of the most wonderful pages in the book he walks, in the Borstal,
from new camp to the Central Block, a mile and a half in his own
company, and reflects, as a Dublinman, not a Dubliner, which is a

different thing, that he had never been in the country much (he was still a boy) except for an odd time training on the Dublin hills with the IRA: that he had never slept a night in any countryside except that flat Suffolk countryside. He missed the Dublin hills which you can see from the city's streets. But the English land was rich and fat and he felt proud of it, and the orchards were shining, and the grain fields, and there was an odd glint of the sea in the distance: and he thought of the Gaelic poet, Brian Merriman, walking out in the County Clare on a morning that would gladden the heart of any man.

Then he came as near as he ever came to composing a hymn:

> I always get grateful and pious in good weather and this was the kind
> of day that you'd know Christ died for you. A bloody good job I
> wasn't born in the South of France or Miami Beach, or I'd be so
> grateful and holy for the sunshine that St Paul of the Cross would be
> only trotting after me, skull and crossbones and all.

So he went on his way whistling Ferguson's 'The Lark in the Clear Air', one of the most enchanting of our love songs. He loved life and he loved the sun. It seems necessary to emphasise this. For not too long before his death a lady from the London *Observer* came over here to write about him: she told me that part of her brief from her editor was to investigate Brendan's death wish and whether or not it was linked to his homosexuality. She asked me about that: and I could only say that, as far as I had ever discerned, there was no death wish. Brendan had a diabetic condition and a long-established taste for drink, two hard-mouthed horses to drive in harness. The diabetes sharpened the taste or the craving; the drink exacerbated the diabetes: the hangovers could only have been Dantean.

Once in my hearing a certain young doctor said to him that he had ten years if he didn't steady and take the treatment. He did neither except for spells and then only under the strong and loving guidance of Beatrice. As it happened he lasted twelve years, but the last year scarcely counted.

His own best comment on this business of the death wish would have been to say that bad as this life could be, the undiscovered country that lay beyond it did not offer much more hope of entertainment. Those who should know best, the padres and even the popes, did not seem in any great hurry to venture out. That argument he often touched on. On the day of Terry Ward's funeral I heard him deal with it more elaborately. Terry, a great journalist, was buried in Skerries on the sea coast of north County Dublin. A party of his friends travelled out from Eden Quay in the city on the upper deck of a bus: a gloomy party setting out, and Brendan had no time for gloom. So, in his most hilarious fashion, he put forward his theory of the afterlife and, before we got ten miles out to the village of Swords, he had us all laughing at Death.

The then pope, Pius XII, had been for some time dying and recovering once a week: which reinforced Brendan's argument. As for himself, he said, the way he wanted to die was to be three months in bed, quite comfortable if declining, and stoutly resisting the advances of the clergy. Then, relenting, he would accept their administrations and die, reunited with Mother Church, and surrounded by relatives and friends all praising the Lord as Brendan is borne aloft by angels. It didn't happen quite that way but the angels may very well have been in attendance.

As for the homosexuality: we've had a lot about that in a sad book by Peter Arthurs: more sad, I feel, for Peter than for Brendan. The only story I could offer to the lady from the *Observer* was that early one sunny morning Brendan and myself left my home, then in Rathgar, and walked down Rathgar Road towards Rathmines. The city went before us, as the folk-tales would have it, and the mountains came behind us, the laburnum and lilac were out and the birds were singing and Dublin was very beautiful: and we were bound for the pubs in the markets beyond the Liffey.

Most reasonably, he was discussing homosexuality. He said that it didn't matter to me because my natural or unnatural bent (apt word) was not that way: and also I had never been to prison nor on board ship as a worker for a long stretch. 'But . . .' said he: and walking ahead of us there was a very handsome fifteen-year-old boy. 'But, would you rather fuck him or . . .' Mentioning a middle-aged lady internationally known for her good works but, God bless and rest her, of a most formidable appearance. His laughter disturbed the birds. It was his *reductio* of a wearying problem out of which the world, either from a medieval or modern approach, has always made too much. Every cripple has his own way of walking, every tinker has his own way of whistling. Let every man, he would have said, walk or whistle his own way, provided he doesn't harm the neighbours or the neighbour's children. He had a great kindly way with children.

To write a book about any man given to drink and to write down only what he did or said when halfway to the horrors is scarcely to give a balanced estimate of the man. For twenty years I enjoyed his friendship and found little in him to sully his humanity, humour and generosity.

Only a man who truly loved his fellow men could have, in the limited spaces of two prisons and a Borstal, found such a field full of folk and made them so memorable. My favourites will always be Chewlips and that mythological Callan from Monaghan who could drill armies and play the bagpipes without moving his lips. There are the brief enigmatic appearances, just to hint to us that we may not after all be on the coral island, of the scarpering boy who pushed his crippled brother over a cliff, or of Gordon who killed his father with a hatchet, or of that fine young man, Heath, who wouldn't wear filthy talk. It says much for Brendan's artistic restraint that he does not tell us how Heath was afterwards to make his mark in life. It was not, I rush to explain, as Prime Minister of the United Kingdom.

Then there was another day in my own home, that time in Dollymount, Clontarf. He picked from my desk a copy, which I was reviewing, of the Turkus-Federman book on Crime, Inc. He leafed through it. He said: 'I'll take this.' He said: 'I've known murderers. I've slept in the room with murderers. But I never, so help me, heard of the like of this.' So he took the book and never brought it back: but the review was finished and I had no urgent wish to reread.

One must, I suppose, mention the episode with Malcolm Muggeridge on the BBC. Some think that Brendan's appearance, peloothered and speechless, before the TV cameras and in the company of Grandmother Muggeridge, helped to launch *The Quare Fellow* on the London stage: that, and the capital punishment debate and, of course, the genius of Joan Littlewood and the lyrical praise from Kenneth Tynan. It's an arguable point. It certainly gave the trash newspapers a happy time following the wild Irishman holding on to the lampposts in Fleet Street and with a constitutional incapacity for keeping (when in his cups) his navel covered.

That last happy phrase I owe to the late George Rogers, a legal man of Omagh, County Tyrone: and dear elder friend of my boyhood. He and Brendan had met in London and discovered that they had a friend in common.

Brendan himself was often foolish enough to argue that any publicity was good publicity. Samuel Johnson put the matter with more wisdom, and restraint.

The BBC unwittingly was to blame. To leave a man, basically a shy man who had already had a few rozzeners to get up his nerve, to leave him alone in a waiting-room with a bottle of Scotch, was to run risks. Afterwards Mr Muggeridge said that Behan was a bore. Since Behan was speechless, it is difficult to see how he could have been a bore, except insofar as all drunk men tend to bore. Without the assistance of alcohol Mr Muggeridge managed all his life to sustain a fair level of boredom.

But as a consequence of all that, I recall a happy and humorous incident. One day, in Mooney's at Baggot Street Bridge (as it then was), Patrick Kavanagh showed me a letter. It was from Father Agnellus Andrews, OFM Director of Religious Programmes for the BBC. It said: 'Dear Mr Kavanagh: We thank you for submitting your two radio plays, *The Priest's Bhoy* and *Get a Mass Said for Yourself*. They are now under consideration. Yours, etc.'

'What,' I said to Paddy, 'did you do?'

'I wrote back,' he said, 'and I told Father Agnellus that if he consulted the Director of Drunken Television, he would find out who wrote those plays and sent them to him over my name.'

It was an earlier practical joke that caused the rift between the poet and the playwright: or was it simply that Baggot Street was not long enough, heaven high enough, nor hell hot enough, to accommodate at the same time two such extraordinary extroverts. My heart and memory hold a warm place for the two of them.

After 1916 George Moore asked: What was General Maxwell* to do, give the rebels prizes for good conduct?

That was not a remark calculated to endear him to the patriots of that or any other time: and we must here remember that Brendan was not in Borstal for being a good boy in his Sunday suit, and that, by

---

* Maxwell was the British Officer in command at Dublin at the time: and under his authority, and under what would have been known as the Rules of War, the executions of the Rebels were carried out.

and large and because of his age, he got off easy, and that he was afterwards confined in Ireland for taking some part in what could only be regarded as a dubious affray. Unless you are an ardent supporter of that curious organisation, Noraid, you may, in these times, be given pause by the nature of the folly that landed him in the hands of the police. He would not wish here, were he alive, to put forward anything in extenuation: he was an Irish Republican as all belonging to him were and had been, and England was the enemy and he was acting off his own bat, and that was that. It is a simple creed: gone now gangrenous as is the way with many things that have been around for too long.

In a TV interview Beatrice Behan was asked if Brendan were alive now what would be his attitude towards the Provisional IRA. It was neither a fair nor a sensible question and Beatrice could only repeat the answer Brendan made to a somewhat similar question when, long before the horrors commenced, it was put to him by a New York journalist: 'Can the leopard change his spots?' Yet I cannot feel that Brendan would be happy in the company of men who would murder a seventeen-year-old boy and then say calmly that the bomb was meant for his father: or who have claimed what they call 'responsibility' for appalling acts of blood. Brendan was first and foremost a great human being, and his description of Lavery would seem to indicate that he was beginning to have doubts about the humanity of some of his comrades-in-arms.

When he was in jail Barnes and Richards were executed for the Coventry bombing. It is almost certain that one of them, at least, was innocent. Brendan claimed that he knew the man who planted the bomb and that it was neither Barnes nor McCormick: and I have heard other men of the then IRA make the same claim. He accepted their end with fatalistic reasonableness:

'I could see the logic of saying to any IRA man, "You may not be the one that planted this bomb, but you have planted others and anyway you are all in this conspiracy together and if we can't get the ones that caused this explosion you'll bloody well do as well as the next, whether you knew they were going to let this bomb off at such a time and at such a place or not." I could see the logic of it, even if they applied it to myself, which God forbid – I considered my present ration of suffering quite adequate – but where any country might do that – and the Irish in the Civil War had no room to talk about death sentences – only England would shove on all this old insulting hypocrisy and tell you in the next breath that they were desperately careful that every foreigner the world over should know that justice had been done according to law.'

When in 1968 the bodies of Barnes and Richards were brought to Ireland for reburial, this present writer walked in the funeral. Indeed, looking back, it would seem that that sad event (British Home Office consenting) was, along with the destruction of Nelson Pillar, a symbolic curtain-raiser for all that has happened since.

In 1965 I wrote down my favourite picture of the man, happy and at home:

> As a great swimmer, next to the sunshine he loved the sea: the eastern sea at the Forty Foot, the swimming-pool famed in *Ulysses*; the laughter of the western Galway sea which, according to Louis MacNeice, juggled with spars and bones irresponsibly. Brendan did not view it so sombrely. On the Aran Islands, and along the Connemara shore, and in Glenties in Donegal with the Boyles and the Harveys, he claimed he could forget all the cruel things of this world. He wrote so pleasantly of the night, after the licensed hours, in the pub in Ballyferriter in Kerry, in the South-west, when the Civic Guards obligingly sent word that they were going to raid, so that the customers could withdraw a little up the mountain slope, taking supplies with them, and drink in peace until the raid was over: 'It was a lovely starlit night and warm, too: and one of my most cherished recollections is of sitting out there on the side of Mount Brandon, looking at the mountain opposite called the Three Sisters framed against the clear moonlit sky and the quiet shimmering Atlantic, a pint of the creamiest Guinness in my hand as I conversed in quiet Irish with a couple of local farmers.'

That was a happy Irishman at home in Ireland. Mount Brandon, as he said with proprietary pride, was called after his patron saint, Brendan the Navigator, who, the legend says, reached the New World before either Norsemen or Columbus, and who left to all who came after him the promise of the Isle of the Blest that all mariners might one day find haven.

'And that,' as Brendan said when he finished his sketch-book,

Brendan Behan's Island, about the island of Ireland, 'is the end of my story and all I'm going to tell you, and thanks for coming along.'

TWENTY-FIVE

By Shannon's Water

That old bilingual wall-map of Ireland that used, in the days of my boyhood, to be on view in schoolrooms, even in the Six Counties, I saw again recently: each of the Thirty-two Counties a distinct colour and no indication at all of the line (it is still called the Border) that cuts off the Six from the Twenty-six. The counties may, in the days of Chichester, the Great Robber, and that pious sycophant, Sir John Davies, have been artificial, arbitrary divisions, but they have settled by now. One of the few divisions or delimitations in this country that have settled or that we might agree about. And on that old map, at any rate, the counties made a pattern that any abstract painter might be proud of: a coloured pattern, coloured counties. And a verse not about our Irish counties but about the counties of the neighbouring island came into my head:

> Here of a Sunday morning
> My love and I would lie,
> And see the coloured counties,
> And hear the larks so high
> Above us in the sky. . . .

But that was Housman's Shropshire Lad and his lass on Bredon Hill. And the lines were displaced on my tongue by less elegant, less romantic, but more comic lines that have for me a closer connection with that old map:

Before the year of 'Ninety-eight
Decided Ireland's wayward fate,
When laws of Death and Transportation
Were served like banquets through the nation. . . .
But let it pass. The tale I dwell on
Has naught to do with red rebellion.
Although it was a glorious ruction
And nearly wrought our foes' destruction,
There lived and died in Limerick City
A dame of fame. Oh, what a pity
That dames of fame should live and die
And never know for what or why. . . .

Which is, as you know, the beginning of the Bard of Thomond's celebrated ballad-story of Drunken Thady who sobered up when he met, high above the River Shannon, the ghost of that dame of fame who, in life, had been a bishop's lady and whose name may, or may not have been, Brady or O'Grady.

The last time I looked on a copy of that old map I was in Limerick City in the company of a dear friend, the city librarian, the never-to-be-forgotten Robert Herbert, who was, among other things, the greatest authority ever on the works of Hogan, the Bard of Thomond. Robert Herbert, tall and bony, with the beard and visage of Don Quixote and a sense of humour like crazy, and a tongue that at times could be as exact as, I have heard, that of James McNeill Whistler.

Overwhelmed by books in his office in the great library he found time to write for the *Limerick Leader* the series of articles, 'Worthies of Thomond', which were afterwards collected in book form. And he talked of everything and everybody, from Johnny Connell who stood up straight, in every bone he was complate, he would throw a stone of any weight from Garryowen to Thomond Gate. To the splendid description of Garryowen at the beginning of Gerald Griffin's novel, *The Collegians*:

Owen's garden was the general rendezvous for those who sought for simple amusement or for dissipation. The old people drank together under the shade of trees – the young played at goal-ball or other athletic exercises on the green, while a few, lingering by the hedgerows with their fair acquaintances, cheated the time with sounds less boisterous, indeed, but yet possessing their fascination.

The festivities of our fathers, however, were frequently distinguished by so fierce a character of mirth that, for any difference in the result of their convivial meetings, they might have been pitched encounters. Owen's garden was soon as famous for scenes of strife as it was for mirth and humour, and broken heads became a staple article of manufacture in the neighbourhood.

For Bob Herbert and myself, and many of our generation, Gerald Griffin and *The Collegians* and Garryowen came to us, for the first time and even the second time, in a second-hand or third-hand way. In my case it was with a group of local amateur players doing Boucicault's *The Colleen Bawn* in the Forester's Hall in Omagh Town. And, next time round, with a week of Opera-Opera in the town hall from O'Meara's travelling company who brought with them the Lily of Killarney. Who else? And where else should a Lily come from.

Were O'Meara's the last people ever to wander the roads of Ireland with a caravan loaded with operas? That week they spent in the town hall was better for me, and many others, than two years at school: Balfe and Jules Benedict and Mephistopheles, and 'La Donna e Mobile' in the *Sacs-Béarla*, and the Daughter of the Regiment flouncing up and down the stage. She really killed us did the Daughter of the Regiment, flouncing specially for a school matinee i.e. an afternoon performance. We whooped every time she flounced, and did a U-bend or a lightning twist. And Dick Minnis, a tall heavily built Canadian who, for some reason or other, was going to school with us, sat on his schoolbag (we had just left the classroom) to get a better view, and the crunch of the collapsing tin box of his mathematical-set was heard above the music and the singing. Opera, opera, as William Saroyan might have said. And the Lily of Killarney was present with the smile of forgiveness softly stealing o'er her beautiful face.

Eily mavourneen, Hardress sang. . . .

He was, I remember, bald on top, which was blindingly noticeable when he went on one knee.

Eily, mavourneen, I see thee before me,
Fairer than ever with Death's pallid hue. . . .

Death's pallid hue, I fear, never made anybody look more fair. And looking at the old map I remembered the laughter of Herbert and myself at our memory of such things. And I remembered, also, a story that I never did or could tell him while he was alive. For once in those days I was showing an American visitor around the scenic beauties of the Glen of Aherlow. This was how I set about it.

He was a man by the name of Kevin Sullivan, a distinguished professor in Columbia and he had written notably about James Joyce among the Jesuits. He was also, God help him and rest him, one of the closest friends I ever had. He had heard a lot about Robert Herbert, the great librarian, and wanted to meet him. So we set off for Limerick City. It was the second journey on which I acted as guide for the distinguished Dr Sullivan. The first journey I had recalled, or used, in a story called 'The Dogs in the Great Glen'. It had brought us to the farthest end of Glencar in Kerry to encounter and meet and be welcomed by Sullivan's grand-uncle. And once the old man stepped forth to welcome us, to be danced around in welcome by his gathering of sheepdogs who, up to that moment, had trotted, watchfully and quietly suspicious, at our heels. That was the way a learned cleric and Kerryman had once told me well-trained dogs behaved in those beautiful but remote, mountainy places.

What happened to you, I wondered, if you were not recognised and welcomed.

But here is how I managed the later journey to introduce Sullivan to Herbert and, on the way, to surprise and even startle him with the Glen of Aherlow. Where my father's father's people came from: my own great-grandfather from a place called Lisvernane. It's still there.

He was a tough man to startle was Sullivan. But I managed to do so. This was how.

From the heart of Tipperary Town there was then, and still is, a quiet unassuming road that led you, tall trees on either hand, and convinced you that you were going nowhere: just through quietude and trees. The Road to Nowhere. Maurice Walsh wrote a book with that title. Nowadays that road is not completely anonymous. There's a signpost in Tipperary Town. But it was not there when I directed Sullivan and he, as a lot of Americans could not help doing, driving on the wrong side of the road. And I assured him the road was a short cut to Limerick City. It may be or have been. I never measured it. It was a narrow road. We met little or no traffic.

Up and up. Trees on either side of us and quietly bending above us. Then a sudden twist, a brief steep ascent and the Wonderland hit you in the face: the great Glen and the Galtee Mountains beyond. The view from Mount Thabor.

Sullivan was shaken. He said that, by God or Somebody, I had sprung this on him and, and. . . .

But I bought him a Black Bushmills in the Glen Hotel, which is still there and splendid, and we renewed our friendship. The sun blessed us. On we went and slowly downward towards the Shannon land. But we made a few more stops. There were hospitable houses by the wayside and pleasant, talkative men within. They delayed us. We were easily persuaded. The skies darkened. When we left Galbally and headed for Limerick City to pay our respects to Robert Herbert, the heavens opened and the rain came down in sheets, shaking the car on the road. Visibility was poor. We overtook a man on an autocycle, rod and net and gaff or something strapped on his back: and, as we did so, we struck a puddle or a minor lake that the storm had made, and we deluged the man from head to toe with dirty water.

'What do we do?' says the polite American

'Drive on,' I said. 'Don't stop to apologise. He'll do us with the gaff.'

So on we drove and stopped for one drink in a Limerick hotel. Then round to the fine stone house beside the library in Pery Square to pay our respects. Much ringing and knocking, and the door opening slowly and the head of a very angry Don Quixote emerging. I am recognised. We are admitted. He is in vest and long drawers, a towel in his hand, his hair and beard in chaos.

'Some gentleman,' he says, 'in a motor, thoroughly drenched me on my road back from fishing in the Mulcaire River.'

His words were not quite as polite as that. He spoke well on the matter for another ten minutes. With the muddy water in his eyes he had identified nothing or nobody. We did not tell him then nor did I afterwards ever tell him. For there were times, as I've said, when he had a tongue as exact as that of James McNeill Whistler. But it is odd the things that come back into your head when you're simply looking at an old map.

EPILOGUE

The Miscellanials

> From quiet homes and first beginning,
> Out to the undiscovered ends,
> There's nothing worth the wear of winning
> But laughter and the love of friends. . . .

And there I go again quoting from memory. But that, anyway, may be the best and friendliest way to quote, for it avoids the formalities of finding and unshelving a book, and fixing on your slippery spectacles and searching for the index, or the contents and the correct page.

And those four lines by Hilaire Belloc are dear to my memory because my good friend, the late Sean J. White, was devoted to and frequently quoted them. And although there is a melancholy in quoting them, now that he is no longer with us, there is also a resonance and many happy memories. The last time I quoted them out loud was during the sad solemnity of his funeral and I felt he was listening and adding his voice to mine.

The next four lines I did not quote for they most certainly did not suit that solemn occasion. But Sean and myself and a group of good friends used to enjoy them and, occasionally, thunder them out. Here they are:

> We taught the art of writing things
> On men we still would like to throttle.
> And where to get the blood of Kings
> At only half-a-crown a bottle. . . .

Regrettably, since the days of Belloc, Kings had become less plentiful and the price of the blood of Kings had ascended. But the group of singing friends that included Sean White and myself faced up bravely to the changing world. We were called, or we called ourselves, The Miscellanials. And this was the origin of that title.

Maxwell Sweeney, an eminent journalist and radio personality, had invented a talk-programme called *Sunday Morning Miscellany*. He ran it for a while, then passed the management of it on to Ronnie Walsh, a noted stage-actor, who kept it going until his retirement some years ago. The programme still functions.

But in the dining-room of the Clarence Hotel on the Dublin Liffeyside a group of friends began to meet for a merry lunch well sustained by the Blood of Kings. That dining-room already had for me, as I may earlier have mentioned, happy associations. For one: it was there I used frequently to meet Father Senan Moynihan, the great Capuchin, and there he introduced me to John Count McCormack. Senan's editorial offices for the *Capuchin Annual*, the *Father Mathew Record*, and the quarterly *Bonaventura*, to all of which I contributed, was just across the Liffey water, by the aid of a bridge, and in Capel Street. Senan was a gentleman and generous and paid well, and had patrons who enabled him to do so.

But about that merry group who met for lunch: it began with a nucleus of Sean White; Anthony O'Riordan, a higher civil servant; Brian Fallon, distinguished journalist and son of the poet, Pádraic Fallon. And John Ryan, author, painter, great editor of literary magazines. And mine humble self. And because we had all contributed to *Sunday Morning Miscellany* it was fated that we should call ourselves The Miscellanials. And all who joined us accepted the name. What a list I could make.

No, it was never just a gathering of various gentlemen. Ladies were invited and treated with courtesy, and enjoyed themselves. There was Barbara Hayley, professor and authority on Carleton and other matters. Tempers were at ease, no swords clashed, and no gentlemen put the bottle to his head. Friends came from across the Atlantic, a notable Flanagan and a notable Sullivan, and a D'arcy O'Brien and the diplomat, George Dempsey. And they came from Paris Herself and other towns.

And the other day, I, a survivor, descended in St Stephen's Green, to a delightful little basement restaurant to join with Brian Fallon, and a gentleman American by the name of Dempsey, and the painter, Stephen MacKenna, and to realise that the Miscellanials were still alive, and laughter and the love of friends.

Glossary

Craobh Rua: Red Branch
Dinnseanchas: Topography
Feis Cheoil: Music festival
Go flúirseach: A-plenty
An Lár: City centre
Sacs-Béarla: English, literally Saxon-English [slang usage]

Index

Works by Benedict Kiely appear directly under title; works by others under author's name